CONSUMER

from a communication, marketing and advertising perspective

Edited by
Sefer DARICI, PhD
ISBN: 978-83-66675-23-0

Sciendo

Print ISBN: 978-83-66675-23-0
Online ISBN: 978-83-66675-24-7
Epub ISBN: 978-83-66675-25-4

Cover Design: Cemre DEMİRÖZ
artcemred@gmail.com

Copyright ©   Sefer DARICI, PhD / Sciendo 2020
sdarici@cumhuriyet.edu.tr

All rights reserved. Without limiting the rights under copyright reserved above, no part of this book may be reproduced, stored in or introduced into a retrieval system, or transmitted, in any form or by any means (electronic, mechanical, photocopying, recording or otherwise) without the written permission of both the copyright owner and the author of the book.

PREFACE

This book contains different perspectives on the consumer from communication, marketing, and advertising perspective. The chapters, each of which is prepared by academicians who are experts in their fields, touch upon the most prominent issues regarding the consumer today.

Each section sheds light on a different point in its field regarding the consumer. It is known that consumption patterns and consumer behaviors have undergone great changes today. The challenges, opportunities, and changes brought about by this change are among the most discussed topics in the literature. In this book, attention is focused on such prominent points.

We hope that the book will bring a different perspective to both the literature and related sectors. I would like to take this opportunity to thank all of our section writers who contributed.

SEFER DARICI, PhD

CONTENTS

Preface
    Sefer DARICI

CHAPTER 1. Brand Activism in The New Media Age: USA and Turkey Samples..1

    Aysel ÇETINKAYA
    Zeynep Benan DONDURUCU
    Gamze Yetkin CILIZOĞLU

CHAPTER 2. Service Failure and Service Recovery in The Context of Customer Relations and Communication........................37

    Derya Fatma BİÇER

CHAPTER 3. The Role of Social Media On Tourism Marketing.........60

    Didem DEMİR.

CHAPTER 4. Advertising Posters and Communication Through Metahors...77

    İbrahim Gökhan CEYLAN

CHAPTER 5. Current Trends in Integrated Marketing Communication..90

    Selçuk Yasin YILDIZ

CHAPTER 6. The Role of Smart Packaging in Communicating with The Consumer 109

    Hatice Bahattin CEYLAN

https://doi.org/10.2478/9788366675247-toc

CHAPTER 1

BRAND ACTIVISM IN THE NEW MEDIA AGE: USA AND TURKEY SAMPLES

Aysel ÇETİNKAYA
Asst. Prof.
Kocaeli University, Deparmant of Journalism
ayselctnky@gmail.com
orcid.org/ 0000-0003-2526-323X

Zeynep Benan DONDURUCU
Res. Asst., Dr.
Kocaeli University, Deparmant of Public Relations and Publicity
zdondurucu@yahoo.com
orcid.org/0000-0002-2634-1001

Gamze Yetkin CILIZOĞLU
Assoc. Prof. Dr.
Kocaeli University, Deparmant of Advertising
yetkingamzec@yahoo.com
orcid.org/0000-0003-0149-034X

Abstract

Brand activism is a new marketing strategy in today's changing society. Many companies are adding activist messages to their social media messages and adapting organizational practices according to changing consumer demands for being more sensitive and responsible about community issues. So, ensuring the credibility of brand activism is important for marketing success as well as accurately drawing has the same importance for its definitional frame that is on the forefront in terms of academic research and for the activities to be planned correctly. Therefore, the concept of brand activism, its main characteristics, and typological classification are examined in this study. After that, in Turkey and the US, brand activism based on social media platforms has been examined within the framework of branding strategies and typological differences, in 2020. Based on the descriptive analysis methodolgy, Kotler and Sarkar's (2018) classification of brand activism strategies and Vrendenburg's et al., (2020) brand activism typology is selected as baseline of the study. In this research results, it is found out that social media

https://doi.org/10.2478/9788366675247-001

sharings by different brands in Turkey and USA includes brand activism strategy due to consumer demand for the operation of taking a stand on social issues. Although the socio-political structure in Turkey makes it difficult for brands to participate in activist movements, this study indicates that Turkish companies are acting sensitive to controversial and diversive issues in Turkey by social maedia. Also, the most important finding of the study is, especially U.S.A brands are mostly adapting an authentic brand activism tactic. So, examined brands present their efforts to frame the problems experienced in society and find solutions to them in social media with a high activist message strategy shows that they have a pro-social brand aim.

Key Words: Social Media, Brand Activism, Brand Communication, New Media

Introduction

In today's market, consumers demand brands to assume stances regarding sociopolitical matters. Brands galvanize social change and profit concerning brand value, joining to brand activism in its real sense when they fuse their activist messages, goals, and values with prosocial corporate implementations. Brand activism is a marketing strategy that is employed by brands that seek to outperform others in markets with high competition, assuming a public stance in social and political matters (Moorman 2020; Sarkar & Kotler, 2018). After the iconized 2018 Colin Kaepernick "Dream Crazy" campaign that took place, during the Black Lives Matter 2020 protests which have started in the USA and spread all over the world many brands have added new strategies to their messaging strategies to set their responses forward against racial discrimination. This disposition of the brands won the support and praise of some, while also receiving criticism from others. Brands tackling polemical and polarizing sociopolitical matters ranging from sexual assault, systematic racism, public health, LGBTQIA+ rights, reproductive health rights, gun control, to immigration, might alienate some consumers (Dodd & Supa, 2014; Korschun and others, 2019; Moorman, 2020; Nalick and others, 2016; Smith & Korschun, 2018; Wettstein & Baur, 2016).

There are also opinions that brand activism has the risk of interrupting the profit and decreasing the brand value and losing the customers' trust when they occupy themselves with activism (Du, Bhattacharya & You, 2010; Alhouti, Johnson & Holloway, 2016; Vredenburg and the rest, 2018). To exemplify the negative effects of brand activism, when Starbucks announced they will hire 10000 Syrian refugees during the refugee debates were heated in the USA, on the ground of this announcement Starbucks faced a two-thirds decrease in "YouGov -BrandIndex's Buzz Score". In addition to that, after the announcement, 30 % of the consumers have stated that they had concerns about buying coffee from the chain store (Marzilli, 2017). The USA based Patagonia which sells outdoor sports products can be cited among brands that succeed in identifying themselves as activist brands. The business donates 1% of their sales to groups related to environmental activities and the themes they focus on are environmental problems like protecting natural habitats, preventing the destruction of forests and rivers, protecting endangered species, the soil, and oceans, and so forth. These activities of Patagonia resulted in tripling their profit since 2014 and being ranked as the 6th in World's Most Creative Brands List in 2018 (Viken Tuasan & Hermansen 2019, p. 26-39; Clement, 2020). As can be seen from the examples given because consumers' responses to activism can vary the debates about brand activism's possible benefits and damages to businesses are ongoing today (Mukherjee & Althuizen 2018, p. 1-2). However, social request for brands to adopt an attitude in the face of social problems or come up with solutions for them is gradually increasing.

Consumers expect big brands to step into the sociopolitical sphere more nowadays (Hoppner & Vadakkepatt, 2019). In the year 2018, Trust Barometer data reports published by Edelman demonstrate that 64% of consumers' demand company CEOs to adopt an attitude regarding social matters. Additionally, in the report, it is stated that 84 % of participants expect the brand managers to present solutions and suggestions and participate in political debates more in terms of topics like environment, globalization, discrimination, and immigration. In the research, it is concluded that one of every two consumers is among the religious consumers who prefer a brand based on the attitude they adopt in terms of social matters, 67% of participants on a global scale stated that they could try a new brand for the first time depending on their attitude towards a given social problem, while 65% stated they would not prefer a brand when the business remains silent. These "belief-based" consumers constitute 59% of the market in USA, 60% in Japan, 57% in UK, and 54% in Germany (Edelman, 2018a, p. 29; Edelman, 2018b, p. 18; Edelman, 2018c, p. 5, 10). The result of a research carried by Sprout Social in the year 2018 concluded that 66% of consumers believe that brands must take stances on sociopolitical matters (Sprout Social, 2018, p. 3). Depending on the rise of anti-discrimination protests for African-American citizens in the USA, results of Trust Barometer report 2020 made by Edelman reveal that belief based purchase behaviors increased to 60%. Additionally, it is concluded that not only are announcements on racial equality made by brands important for consumers but also are taking action. Being aware of the problem, advocating racial equality, and educating the public are among the expectations of consumers for brands (Edelman, 2020 p. 13-16).

Brands being activists in the sociopolitical sphere has revealed the need to investigate more closely the reasons for its basis (Holt, 2002). Barkley Cause Survey concluded that 66% of firms are actively occupied with goal marketing and that it is also mentioned as institutive sociopolitical activism and/or brand activism (Cause Good, 2018). Marketing academicians (Kotler & Sarkar, 2017; Moorman 2020) and applicators (Unilever 2019a) stress the importance of authenticity in brand activism. In this context, ensuring the credibility of brand activism is important for marketing success as well as accurately drawing has the same importance for its definitional frame that is on the forefront in terms of academic research and for the activities to be planned correctly. Therefore, the concept of brand activism, its main characteristics, and typological classification are examined in this study. In today's world, among the most suitable to carry activist operations are social media channels which have the structure that allows for engagement, a fast and instant engagement for that matter. Research about brand activism carried by Sprout Social in 2018 concluded that consumers think brands should announce their support for any given social problem on social media and consumers themselves should be more active in terms of taking the crucial steps to support this purpose (Sprout Social, 2018, p. 3). Through social media, consumers can rapidly circulate the things they find satisfactory and dissatisfactory about a brand with a simple hashtag, keyword, picture, or words. Considering that two-thirds of generation Y consumers use social media to interact with a given business' social responsibility projects, by announcing the activist practices these businesses increase their opportunities to appeal to consumer values more (Cone Communications, 2015). Depending on the level of interaction social media posts get from other users, engagement metrics are going to rise, brand awareness is going to increase in tandem with the increase in the number of views, a "common cause" between the defended point and the consumers are going to develop from there, and act of buying is going to follow these and it will result in a long-term increase of profit. To exemplify brand activism applications applied on social media, Airbnb initiating the #weaccept movement (which aims to accept and love humans regardless of their roots or countries of origin) which emerged after D. Trump's, President of USA, statements about immigration, and Protect & Gamble's #weseeequal campaign for a world independent of gender inequality within the context of International Women's Day, which they circulated based on social media in 2018 can be cited (Gray, 2019, p. 3-4). Likewise, yogurt brand Yoplait's "mom-on" campaign which criticizes the social pressure on mothers about how to be a good parent can be given as an example for campaigns that aim at brand activism through social media. According to the data taken from Google, this campaign increased the affinity rate towards the brand by 1.4 % (Gilliand, 2018). As can be seen in the examples given, because consumers give more and more value to corporate social responsibility, an ever-increasing number of companies announce to the public, their opinions on social and political matters in society. Research done by Edelman in 2018 and 2019, and the research done by Sprout Social in 2018 reveals consumers believe that social change is conducted better through brands than governments and that brands more easily produce an effect in terms of resolving a social problem. For this reason, it can be said that a properly fabricated brand activism will be effective in solving social matters.

One of the fundamental benefits of brand activism to corporations is having the chance to witness how the activist actions they perform or support are being perceived in society. Because brands can examine the compatibility rate of business values with those of costumers. These days society's increasing expectations for businesses to adopt social matters and come up with solutions for them has caused brand activism acts to gather momentum. Especially the structure of social media platforms which enable an unmediated interaction between the user and the brand offers an opportunity for businesses to determine the right strategies by determining the interaction rate of posts containing activist content created within the context of a given campaign. Despite the increasing participation of foundations in social and political spheres, the research directed to when and how brand activism originated and why it is effective as a strategy is quite limited. To illustrate these studies, Mukherjee and Althuizen's (2018) research about brand activism's pros and cons on businesses that they analyzed based on consumers' political opinions and Shetty et al. (2019) research that concluded brands which embrace social, political, cultural, or environmental problems are approved more by generation Y users, not depending on variables like age, gender, amount of income and so forth, can be given as examples. Moreover, Gray (2019) in her research examining the link between brand activism and social media engagement, concluded that the engagement rate between the businesses which perform brand activism acts on Twitter and their followers have increased. Whereas in Turkey, there is no study investigating brand activism in literature. Based on this deficiency in the body of literature, this study aims to determine the typological properties of the activist actions that brands give place to on social media in Turkey by examining "brand activism" samples both from Turkey and from all around the globe. Thus, with the comparative analysis of social media-based brand activism actions varying from one country to another, this study will form a comprehensive application framework about this new marketing communication (Marcom) strategy which is coming to the forefront more and more around the world.

1. Development of Brand Activism Actions and Differences Between These and Other Marketing Communication Applications

Brand activism is defined as a value-oriented strategy applied by companies to display mindedness about the current and upcoming social qualities. This new strategy is also expressed as the phenomenon of businesses stating their opinions regarding a cause or a problem (Kotler & Sarkar, 2017). Kotler & Sarkar (2018, p. 70), assert that the natural value-driven progress of institutional social responsibility (ISR) actions and the social environment, and managerial development programs are both involved in brand activism. Just as the case for brand activism, there is no exact definition for the concept of institutional social responsibility either. The concept of ISR is a body of applications essentially based on voluntariness and which contains the activities realized by the businesses using their resources to promote social welfare. Additionally, the concept is also defined as a strategy which has commercial and social benefits both (Kotler & Lee, 2008, p. 2-5; McKinsey & Company, 2009; Keys, Malnight & van der Graaf, 2009). The main difference between institutional social responsibility actions and brand activism as stated by Kotler & Sarkar (2018, p. 581) is brand activism focusing on the societal matters which are the most urgent and important at a given time. Generally, brand activism is distinct from ISR in the following two ways. Firstly, ISR puts stress over these actions and their consequences (i.e. reputation, sales) much more than internal business values (Wettstein & Baur, 2016). Secondly, society largely perceives ISR actions beneficiary. On the contrary, brand activism lacks such integrity of opinion because these sociopolitical matters in question do not have a universal "truth" and in some cases, these might not be perceived as a problem (Korschun et al. 2019; Nalick et al. 2016). Consequentially brand activism is an evolved ISR (Sarkar & Kotler, 2018).

Compared to standard marketing campaigns that promote a given product, brand activism campaigns focus on social or political matters. With that being said, there are some campaigns, most of them classified as hybrids, serving a hybrid purpose such as of both advocacy and marketing products

(Drumwright, 1996, p. 76). In this context, the distinction between brand activism and cause-related marketing campaigns should be made precisely (Bruder & Lübeck, 2019, p. 12). Cause-related marketing applications encompasses all of the promotion activities carried by a given business to support a special goal apart from the presentation of products/services and commercial objective (Beise-Zee, 2013, p. 321). Cause-related marketing activities differ from the institutional charity as it connotes businesses donating a part of their revenues, generally aiming at a relief organization or for a goal, and by forming a marketing partnership (Wherry & Schor, 2015, p. 304-305). Cause-related marketing with these features is distinct from brand activism since it is a sales-based donation transfer application. With the advocacy marketing concept, it is defined as the endeavors of operators to influence the public policy formation process to secure the market, as Sethi (1977) indicates it is among the corporate advertising activities since the beginning of the 20th century. Social and political changes taking place in the 1970s induced the increase of advocacy advertising activities.

Advocacy marketing applications are employed to overcome communication barriers with the stakeholder groups and build trust for the right ones in areas with high levels of risk such as coal, gasoline, alcohol, tobacco, and pharmaceutical industries (Miller & Sinclair, 2009, p. 37). The table shown below demonstrates in detail the features of cause-related marketing, corporate social marketing, advocacy advertising, and brand activismpractices.

Table 1. Brand Activism CSR, CRM, Advocacy Advertising Comparison and Core Features

CSR Activity	Cause Promotion and Cause-Related Marketing	Corporate Social Marketing	Advocacy Advertising	Brand Activism
Form	Monetary (advertising included)	Advertising	Advertising	Advertising and practice
Goal	To influence customer understanding through company-cause associations	Seek prestigious and economic gain via consumer approval of association with cause/issue	Evoke organizational change through shifting public opinion and behavior	Support a cause, create awareness, behavior modification and support sociopolitical change; also seeks prestigious and economic gain via consumer appreciation of association with a cause
Driver (Kotler et al. 2012)	Marketing driven	Marketing driven	Marketing driven	Purpose and values-driven
Controversy Degree	Noncontroversial charity, cause, or event	Noncontroversial issue	Noncontroversial issue	Controversial sociopolitical cause, issue, charity, or event
Issue Nature	Progressive	Progressive	Benefit industry	Progressive or conservative
Main Issue	Social, environmental	Social, environmental	Political	Social, political, environmental, legal, business, or economic
Engagement Nature	No/minimal internal practice	Messaging only, no internal practice	Messaging only, no internal practice	Alignment between messaging and practice
Illustrative topics	Red Cross, Breast cancer research, UNICEF	Problems influence the organization's immediate industry	Problems involved with the company's operations, defending themselves from criticism; mainly appears in unsafe business such as oil and tobacco	Gender rights, LGBTQIA rights, immigration, climate change U.S. gun reform etc.

Sample	Pampers donates, a piece of its revenue to UNICEF for a vaccine against neonatal tetanus	Heineken started a "drink responsibly" campaign	R.J. Reynolds (Tobacco Company) disputed the harmfulness of smoking	Gillette's viral advertisement about exploring toxic masculinity
Literature	Kotler, Hessekiel and Lee, 2012; Crimmins and Horn 1996; Varadarajan and Menon 1988	Haley, 1996; Kotler and Lee 2005; Inoue and Kent 2014	Fox 1986; Cutler and Muehling 1989; Menon and Kahn, 2003; Haley 1996	Korschun et al. 2019; Dodd & Supa 2014; Nalick et al. 2016; Moorman, 2020; Smith & Korschun 2018; Sarkar & Kotler 2018; Wettstein & Baur, 2016

(Vrendeburg et al., 2020, p. 3)

As seen in the table above, the most fundamental feature of cause-related marketing is donating a part of the profit obtained from product sales or a portion of the business' profit to a social purpose or charity organization. Conversely, the basic feature of corporate social responsibility practices is generally the implementation of a market-oriented social responsibility campaign related to a problem experienced in their market. In the advocacy advertising style, the company conducts communication activities essentially to have a say on the discussions regarding the product or the service field in which it operates. Advocacy advertising is widely used in industries such as tobacco and petroleum, which are considered to be catastrophic to human health and the environment. Brand activism differs from other communication strategies listed in focusing more on the controversial issues and being goal/value-oriented. Businesses carry out brand activism activities by establishing certain attitudes towards many different and controversial and largely debated social matters.

2. Brand Activism's Features, Strategies Used, and Its Classification

Brand activism emerges when a brand corporately assumes a non-neutral stance on controversial sociopolitical matters aiming to create social change and marketing success. In this case, four prominent features of brand activism are listed as follows: (Vrendenburg et al., 2020, p. 3-4)

1. Brand activism is directed towards a goal and a value.
2. It tackles controversial, debatable, and polarizing sociopolitical matters.
3. The matter may be progressive or conservative by its very nature (problems are often subjective and politics, ideology, religion, and other ideologies/beliefs are prominent in determining them)
4. The brand contributes to the solving of sociopolitical matters by giving social messages and carrying out applications.

Additionally, the key features of brand activism may be listed as having a symbolic value or character, not being directly related to the product or service, creating a reputation-enhancing situation, connecting the target audience to the brand within the framework of emotional motives, as they are associated with social movements and in general have a unique character. Besides, with brand activism businesses break any controversial issue from the conventional political context and build their strategies on core values such as equality and environmental protection. For this reason, brand activism does not support a political party or formation directly.

However, it aims to ensure social progress especially in terms of controversial issues. Additionally, in some cases, there are instances of brand activism advocating conservative values instead of progressive views. Other basic features of brand activism include being global, being nourished by digital roots, and having a hybrid structure. Although brands shape their activism practices through campaigns locally carried, it is seen that the activities of global businesses spread easily to the world with the development of new communication technologies and social media. Brand activism's digitality is defined as its connection with online activism at a global and local level, and the spontaneous interaction resulting from the subject matter advocated by videos and logos. (Manfredi Sanchez, 2019, p. 348-349).

Among the brand activism campaigns that are influential all over the world with the help of digital networks, Procter and Gamble's #Likeagirl campaign, which aims to overcome the gender stereotypes for girls and to encourage them to act confidently, can be given. This campaign which uses YouTube as its main channel has a history of five years. A network analysis study on this viral campaign concluded that although it was higher in the first period of the campaign, this viral campaign achieved high interaction with comments, views, likes, and user-generated tags alike. (Lee and Youn, 2020, p. 156). The table below demonstrates the main characteristics of brand activism:

Table 2. Characteristics of Brand Activism

Attributes	Definition	Brand Activism Links	Sample
Aim and values-driven	Brand purpose is embedded as well as reproduced from its vital values. So, a brand is not only motivated by profit but also focuses on its support to the public interest and collective aims (The British Academy, 2019), Also, the brand prioritizes the society and the environment's benefits (Bocken et al. 2014).	Aim and value-oriented brand activism focus on the effect of socio-political problems beyond urgent economic interests (Sarkar & Kotler, 2018; Wettstein & Baur, 2016).	**Unilever**: 28 "sustainable living" brands: in this sample, brands aimed to reduce environmental footprint and create a social influence (Unilever 2019b). **Tony's Chocolonely**: in this sample, the company constituted a reference sale price for cocoa and aimed to collaborate with other chocolate firms for making a change in the market (Tony's Chocolonely, 2020).
Controversial, Contested, polarizing Socio-political issues	Controversial problems are creating competition between interests and values; cause conflicts about actions and assertions which can be politically delicate, and revive powerful emotions (Flinders University, 2019; Nalick et al., 2016). However, the representation of a contested issue can change by the time and be different in various cultures. Also, the media's presentation of an issue can be effective in public opinion. The current problems in media can be classified as sexual harassment, climate change, equality (gender), racism, gun control, LGBTI rights, and public health.	Brands are preferring and are comfortable with estranging certain customers by engaging with dividing sociopolitical issues (Smith & Korschun 2018).	**Gillette**: in this sample, the brand advertisements are against the toxic masculinity. Also, the company made donations to charities which are addressed toxic masculinity (Al-Muslim, 2019). **Nike**: in this sample, the company's advertisement is attaching importance to Black Lives Matter protestor and ex- NFL football player Colin Kaepernick focuses on racial inequality (Boren, 2018).
Progressive and conservative stances	The espousal of the progressive or conservative position. Both can be thought pro-social as they believe their actions benefit the community (Chatterji and Toffel, 2018; Eisenberg, 1982).	Brand activism can focus on any socio-political problem along with the political division. (This stance can be subjective, based on religion or political ideology) (Moorman, 2020).	**Dick's Sporting Goods**: in this sample, it is seen that the company was a supporter of the U.S. National Rifle Association for a long time. Also, the firm was a purveyor of firearms, so the brand stance was conservative. After the school shooting in Parkland, Florida; the brand outlawed the assault rifles sale in its stores. This ban caused a negative backlash in a conservative customer base. On the other hand, the customers who support gun control were pleased because this action is suitable for their values (Edgecliffe- Johnson, 2018). **Nordstrom**: in this sample, the company decided not to continue President D. Trump's daughter Ivanka Trump's fashion style. So, D. Trump supporters started a social media boycott for the firm. However, the brand has been already boycotted by non-Trump supporters (Creswell & Abrams, 2017).
Practice and messaging	Brand activism contains both abstract (message) and physical (practice) pledge to a sociopolitical issue (Delmas and Burbano, 2011).	Brand activism extends beyond solely advocacy/messaging (i.e., Dodd & Supa, 2014; Nalick et al., 2016; Wettstein & Baur, 2016) and involves organizational actions that encourage brand purpose and values.	**Messaging:** in these messages of CEO statements sample, some CEO's made statements against U.S. President D. Trump ban of immigration (Cohn 2017). In this advertising message sample, **The 2017 Super Bowl commercials** are important for attracting attention to gender, immigration, and environmental issues (WGSN Insider 2017). **Practices:** In this corporate practice sample, **Target** introduced gender-inclusive bathrooms for transgender people (WGSN Insider 2017). Procter & Gamble's guarantee for $3 million donations for Gillette toxic masculinity campaign because of relevant cause can be seen as a support practice (Gillette 2019). Kenco's started a "Coffee vs. Gangs" campaign which aims to create a training program for young men in Honduras for being coffee farmers. This project's purpose is saving youth from being gang members and can be evaluated as continued support practice (Holder, 2017).

(Vrendenburg et al., 2020:4-5)

As seen from the table given above, brand activism is goal and value-oriented, which means that it takes the public benefit as a basis, goes beyond momentary economic interests, and puts social benefit at the focal point. As Moorman (2020) argued in the example of Patagonia, in some cases, this fundamental feature can be considered as established brands carrying some kind of a political mission. Nevertheless, brands can play an educative role with brand activism practices and act more responsibly in the social change process to improve the social structure (Moorman, 2020 quoted by Vrendenburg et al., 2020, p. 5).

Another key feature of brand activism is that it focuses mainly on polarizing, controversial, or contentious matters. Because issues of this nature can lead to conflict and political sensitivity can induce strong feelings. According to Moorman (2020), this situation may cause alienation among some consumer groups since not all consumer groups share the same values and sensitivities.

The third fundamental feature of brand activism is that it is shaped on a stance that can be described as subjective concerning controversial matters. The last feature of brand activism is having both a message-based abstract and application-based concrete features. While the support of consumers, businesses, and stakeholders in the area of advocation rises with messages, the desired attitude can be reflected in the corporate behavior style with the application practices.

Thus, the brand fulfills its mission in the social change process (Vrendenburg et al., 2020, p. 5). In this context, the main benefits of brand activism practices to businesses can be listed as revealing that the business considers social benefit rather than profit, attracting potential customers, employees, and stakeholders, while holding existing stakeholders and customers, and increasing market share (Moorman, 2018)

Brand activism has a five-stage framework consisting of Brand Activism Strategy, Brand Activism Maps, Brand Activism Canvas, The Brand Activism X Matrix, and Brand Activism Scorecard (Sarkar & Kotler, 2018, p. 1469-1476). Sarkar & Kotler (2018, p. 632-636) classify these brand activism strategies as social activism (prevention of discrimination on the ground of age, gender, race or sexual orientation, providing equal rights for and accessibility of education, etc.), legal activism (corporate tax, working conditions, employee rights, etc.), commercial activism (governance, CEO payments, labor and union relations, compensation, management processes, etc.), economic activism (minimum tax and salary payments that can affect inequality and equal distribution of income), political activism (voting rights, election campaigns, lobbying activities, lawmaking, etc.) and environmental activism (environmental issues, use of water resources and land, etc.).

In the second stage, there is the brand activism map and this stage includes mapping the six dimensions of brand activism strategies and determining the problems which come to the forefront. Other stages are Brand Activism Canvas as the business strategy, to evaluate which "value gaps" exist among stakeholders, brand activism X Matrix to make the necessary arrangements to manage initiatives, and Brand Activism Scoreboard, which uses a simple control system or panel to evaluate progress (Sarkar & Kotler, 2018, p. 1469-1476).

After having determined the strategy, whether a progressive or a conservative/regressive attitude regarding the matter will be adopted by the brand should be determined. In this step, setting a regressive position by businesses ignoring the values and needs of the society creates a "value gap". Conversely, determining a "progressive" behavior pattern is an indicator of strong successful leadership (Sarkar and Kotler, 2018, p. 698).

The "common good" theme is the basis of the business's determination of a "progressive" or "regressive" position based on the "value gap". If the business remains in a neutral position, the key benefits of society will not be disturbed. Brand's "progressive activism" applications will help the "common good" by creating "inclusion" while "regressive activism" will create the opposite effect by causing "polarization" (Sarkar and Kotler, 2018, p. 802). The diagram below displays a "typology of brand activism" based on message and application variables.

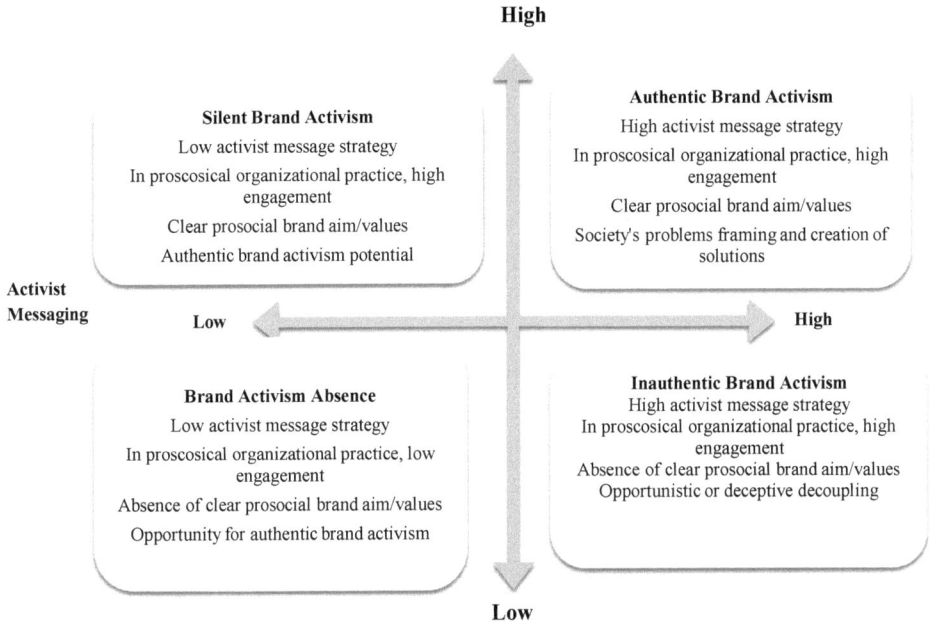

Diagram 1. Brand Activism Typology

Source:(Vrendenburg et al., 2020, p. 6)

In the typology, there are brands in the "Absence of Brand Activism" category in the first quarter. These businesses are brands that have not yet adapted to pro-community corporate practices in their approach to the market and do not have pro-social brand goals or values and which do not use activist marketing messages. They operate without consumer expectations of involvement in brand activism and to ensure brand legitimacy they tend to be located in industries that are not conventionally linked to partnering for sociopolitical reasons. These brands generally operate in the business to business (B2B) sector and perform traditional marketing practices. Caterpillar is an example of businesses that are in the Absence of the Brand Activism stage (Vrendenburg et al., 2020, p. 7). Although companies in this category have problems with activist messages and behavior and they lack value, to create an "authentic" activist brand strategy they can weigh out the opportunities and achieve success.

The brands in the Silent Brand Activism category in the second quarter place sociopolitical reasons based on their strategic focus or mission. These brands are more likely to move quietly behind the scenes by implementing long-term behavioral corporate practices that have become a part of their business style, focusing on core goals and values, and on those which benefit the society. In today's world, such businesses tend to be generally smaller and they tend to engage in activism on controversial matters, holding less brand power in the market. For instance, HoMie, an Australian clothing brand established in Melbourne, by providing revenue, job skills and mentorship aims to save the young from homelessness. Detailed information about the business activities is available at www.homie.com.au. For Silent brand activists operating in the field of sustainability the example of Klean Kanteen can be given, which produces B-Corps with natural product manufacture and reusable food and beverage containers (Vrendenburg et al., 2020, p. 7). The predominant deficiency of brands in this category is that they cannot present their activist message strategies to the public through the right communication channels. However, these businesses can switch to the "authentic" brand activism typology, presenting the values that they have adapted to the corporate behavior culture to the stakeholder groups with the proper promotion strategies.

In the third quarter, some brands fall within the "Authentic Brand Activism" typology. The main reason why these brands are perceived as "authentic" is that they have brand goals and values, activist marketing messages, and corporate applications that aim to benefit society. Examples for these businesses include ice cream manufacturer Ben & Jerry's, shoe brand TOMS, and Patagonia, which sells outdoor sports products. To illustrate, ice cream manufacturer Ben & Jerry's has embraced activism based on economic, social, and product quality values since the 1980s. Ben & Jerry's focus on quality products, its adoption of sustainable food systems, its use of fair trade products, and its opposition to the use of growth hormones in cattle (and purchasing dairy products from farmers' cooperatives) form the basis of its activist brand strategy. The main reasons why "Authentic Brand Activism" is more effective than other forms of brand activism is that activist marketing messages, which act as a catalyst for social change, are carried out in a balanced way with purpose and value-oriented corporate practices and increase brand value. The formation of the brand value of the businesses in this typology is fundamentally tied to the positive positioning of the brand as a result of the activism practices of the potential consumers and the reliable and positive brand associations in their minds. In this type of brand activism that requires a long process, authentic brand activists create brand value for the current campaign increasing the likelihood that future activist campaigns will contribute to brand value. In general, brands that perform "authentic brand activism" adopt a "progressive stance", yet Chick-fil-A, a well-known conservative-Christian fast-food chain, has built its core values and practices on being closed on Sundays and supporting anti-marriage organizations between LGBTI individuals showing an example of "authentic brand activism" (Vrendenburg et al., 2020, p. 7-8). Drawing from this, authentic brand activists can adapt to different situations and perform different activities according to social conditions without leaving their core values and practices.

The "Inauthentic Brand Activism" typology includes the brands in the 4th quarter. While these businesses embrace activist marketing messages that convey their support for sociopolitical causes, such brands lack explicit brand goals and values. Therefore, brands in this category do not implement pro-social corporate practices and hide the absence of these practices. This situation may cause brand activism activities to be perceived as dishonest, unrealistic, and even deceptive. Among the main risks of being in this category is the increased likelihood of being confronted by the consumers due to the increasing demands for transparency and brands which can be held accountable. However, unoriginal brand activism not only causes negative brand equity through negative brand associations and false signals; but also causes these negative effects such as limiting the potential for social change and causing insecurity in the consumer, as it may include misleading and groundless claims. "Inauthentic Brand Activism" works create woke-washing and to these practices, the Pepsi advertising campaign can be given in which Pepsi used TV star Kendall Jenner during the Black Lives Matter (BLM) protests to reach a young target audience in 2017. The advertisement used footage of a peaceful protester confronting the armed units followed by the scenes in which the protest changes into a party with K. Jenner giving a can of Pepsi to one of the armed officers. Ultimately, the advertisement in question was taken down due to the large criticism it received from the consumers and potential consumers alike. In this example, while there are an activist message and a wide target audience, the fact that the business does not have the value and the structure to apply it properly to support this message causes woke-washing (Barton et al., 2018; Vrendenburg et al., 2020, p. 7-8). In this context, although "inauthentic brand activism" seems to benefit businesses in the short term, it harms both the social change processes and consumer confidence and brand value in the long run.

3. Investigation of Brand Activism Activities From Turkey and in the World through Social Media Platforms

In this study, in Turkey and the US, in 2020, brand activism based on social media platforms has been examined within the framework of branding strategies and typological differences.

3.1. Purpose, Sample, Limitations and Method

In this study, it is aimed to determine the strategic and typological characteristics of the activists' activities featured by businesses in social media by examining "brand activism" samples from United States and Turkey. Thus, social media-based brand activism activities will be analyzed comparatively, depending on the countries studied. Thereby, similar and different application forms of this marketing communication strategy according to countries will be revealed.

The sample of the study was determined by purposeful sampling method. Purposeful sampling, which is basically a non-probabilistic sampling method, can be used in special cases and for in-depth research of rich data, depending on the aims of the researcher (Büyüköztürk et al., 2018, p. 92-92; Yıldırım & Şimşek, 2008, p. 107). In the study, due to the limited number of brands that carry out brand activism actions, the shares of brands showing this feature on social media were analyzed. The reason for the limitation of the study to social media platforms is that, as a result of the research conducted by Sprout Social in 2018, consumers' increased expectations from brands to account their support for social problems in social media platforms and requirement of guidance for their followers in supporting a social objective. The reason why the campaigns analyzed in the study are examined on different social media platforms is, as Vrenderburg et al. As (2020, p. 4-6) stated, combined use of message, value, purpose and application areas within the framework of brand activism actions. Besides, as emphasized by Soler and Jimenes (cited in 2012, Manfredi Sanches, 2019, p. 349), it provides the opportunity to compare the data of different resource use in the study of a social phenomenon. The research was limited to the period between January 2020 and August 2020 due to time and cost constraints.

In this study, the descriptive analysis method defined by Dey (1993) as a qualitative research method was used. The data collected in the descriptive analysis method are classified according to specific themes. Thus, a comparison and correlation can be made between the findings at the end of the research. In this way, the similarities, relationships and differences between variables are examined depending on the themes studies; a link can be established between them (Dey, 1993, p. 32-44). Based on the descriptive analysis, Kotler and Sarkar's (2018, p. 632-636) classification of brand activism strategies consisting of social activism, legal activism, commercial activism, economic activism, political activism and environmental activism, and Vrendenburg's et al., (2020, p. 6) brand activism typology which consist of "silent, authentic and inauhentic" activism is selected as baseline. The "brand activism absence" category in this typology is not evaluated for this study, since the brands that carry out activism actions are examined.

3.2. Research Findings

The following table which shows the posts made by brands with brand activism actions in Turkey and the world on social media platforms were analyzed in the framework of the strategic and typological features.

Table 3. Turkey and USA Brands' Social Media Posts Analysis Related with Brand Activism Campaigns in 2020

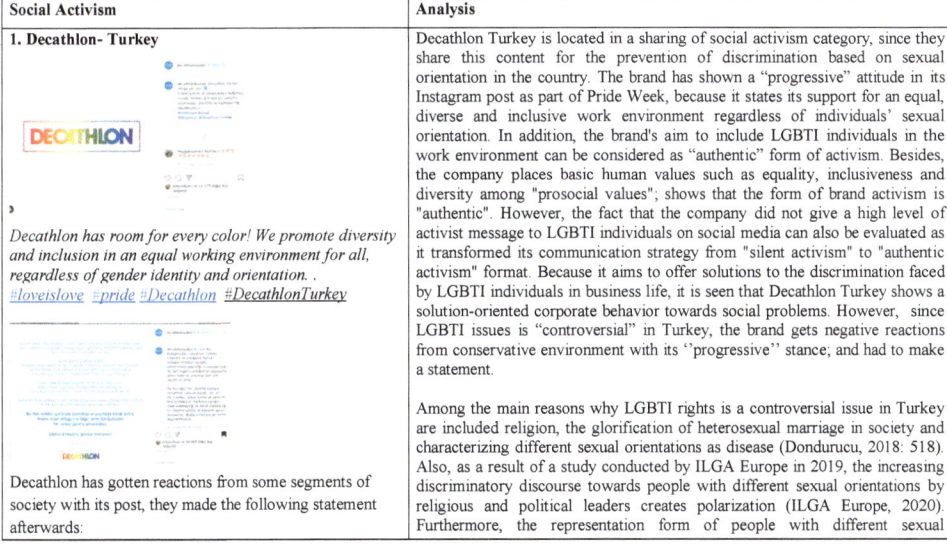

Social Activism	Analysis
1. Decathlon- Turkey *Decathlon has room for every color! We promote diversity and inclusion in an equal working environment for all, regardless of gender identity and orientation. .* *#loveislove #pride #Decathlon #DecathlonTurkey* Decathlon has gotten reactions from some segments of society with its post, they made the following statement afterwards:	Decathlon Turkey is located in a sharing of social activism category, since they share this content for the prevention of discrimination based on sexual orientation in the country. The brand has shown a "progressive" attitude in its Instagram post as part of Pride Week, because it states its support for an equal, diverse and inclusive work environment regardless of individuals' sexual orientation. In addition, the brand's aim to include LGBTI individuals in the work environment can be considered as "authentic" form of activism. Besides, the company places basic human values such as equality, inclusiveness and diversity among "prosocial values"; shows that the form of brand activism is "authentic". However, the fact that the company did not give a high level of activist message to LGBTI individuals on social media can also be evaluated as it transformed its communication strategy from "silent activism" to "authentic activism" format. Because it aims to offer solutions to the discrimination faced by LGBTI individuals in business life, it is seen that Decathlon Turkey shows a solution-oriented corporate behavior towards social problems. However, since LGBTI issues is "controversial" in Turkey, the brand gets negative reactions from conservative environment with its ''progressive'' stance; and had to make a statement. Among the main reasons why LGBTI rights is a controversial issue in Turkey are included religion, the glorification of heterosexual marriage in society and characterizing different sexual orientations as disease (Dondurucu, 2018: 518). Also, as a result of a study conducted by ILGA Europe in 2019, the increasing discriminatory discourse towards people with different sexual orientations by religious and political leaders creates polarization (ILGA Europe, 2020). Furthermore, the representation form of people with different sexual

CONSUMER

As part of Pride Month, the post we share from our Decathlon Turkey Linkedin and Instagram account about diversity and inclusiveness of our work environment got reactions and comments which surprised and upset us very much. We are against all kinds of discrimination. As Decathlon Turkey; we have an environment where everyone can express themselves and be themselves, regardless of religion, language, race, gender, gender identity and orientation, and we are proud of it. We cannot think of any other way. As stated in the Universal Declaration of Human Rights, "All human beings are born free and equal in dignity and rights". No company, individual or even any force can take this right away from people. We invite everyone to be more sensitive and inclusive these days, when we see how discrimination is driving the world into chaos in different ways. We always proudly stand behind our stance, which embraces all colors and embraces diversity and values people because they are human. We believe in the unifying power of sport!	orientations in the mass media and the user-centered structure of social media channels also accelerate the discussions against LGBTI individuals, especially during Pride Week celebrations.
2. Koç Holding-Turkey	Koç Holding Turkey express its support for the Istanbul Convention on violence against women through the content shared on its Twitter page. The Istanbul Convention is an international human rights convention that determines the basic standards and obligations of states in the field of violence against women and domestic violence. It was opened for signature in Istanbul on 11 May 2011; then entered into force in 2014. Signed by 46 countries and the European Union as of July 2020, it was ratified in 32 of the signatory countries (Council of Europe, 2020). The contract that Turkey has also signed, due to the increase of violence against women and killings of women in the country, has entered the debate among the issues that society discusses. The main thesis of the groups opposed to the Istanbul Convention is the view that the concepts of "sexual orientation" and "gender" in the convention are not suitable for the Turkish family structure. In addition, this group claims that LGBTI and some marginal formations threaten future generations. The main thesis of the supporters of the convention is that with this agreement, it is aimed to protect women's right to life and to increase their social status (AA, 2020).
[Koç Holding tweet image] *Violence against women is a violation of human rights. Being a party to the Istanbul Convention is an indication of determination to combat violence against women. On this occasion, we invite everyone and all authorized institutions in our country to protect and adhere to the Istanbul Convention. We believe that it is necessary to struggle in solidarity for a country where women are not subjected to violence and killed. As Koç Group, we will continue to focus on particularly elimination of violence against women as it has been until today as well as to work for a world where women have equal rights and freedoms with men.*	Koç Holding has taken a "progressive" attitude on this subject, which is highly controversial in the society, and has used an activist message approach in its sharing. Koç Holding has some projects on women's rights and women's equality in social / business life. These projects include "I Support Gender Equality for My Country" covering the period between 2015-2017, and "HeforShe", which calls men to defend women's rights from the UN Gender Equality and Women's Empowerment Unit "UN Women" (Koç Sistem, 2020). In this context, it shows that Koç Holding, as a corporate behavior style, supports projects aimed at ensuring equality in participation in social life and conducts "authentic brand activism" activities with the activist message strategy for the Istanbul Convention.
3. Nike-ABD	The content is in the social activism category as Nike made an Instagram post on the prevention of discrimination against African American citizens in the

CONSUMER

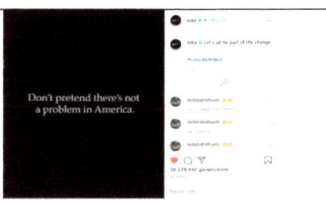

The For Once, Don't Do It' Don't pretend there's not a problem in America. Don't turn your back on racism. Don't accept innocent lives being taken from us. Don't make any more excuses. Don't think this doesn't affect you. Don't sit back and be silent. Don't think you can't be part of the change. Let's all be part of the change.

"Believe in something. Even if it means sacrificing everything,"

USA. The brand carried out this sharing to support the serial anti-racist protests that were linked to the murder of a black citizen, George Floyd, as a result of police violence, in Minneapolis on May 26. The George Floyd protests have also become part of the Black Lives Matter movement, spreading over 2,000 cities, towns and 60 countries. During the period of June, July and August 2020, these protests; as it is estimated that 15-26 million people attend ; seen as the biggest protest in the history of the country. The reasons of the growing protests in the country and the fact that they have become a contentious issue can be listed as the use of disproportionate use of force by the police, the revolt of demonstrations in cities such as Chicago, the harsh governing of the US President Trump, the military intervention and the effective use of social media by demonstrators. (Taylor, 2020, Carrega & Lloyd, 2020, Wikipedia, 2020).

It is observed that Nike has taken a "progressive" attitude with its Instagram sharing regarding the subject that has a "polarizing" feature in the country. Nike's open support for the anti-racist movement started to gain an "activist" feature together with the beginning of radical protests in the games of American Football League player Colin Kaepernick in 2018 and the spread of this situation to the sports community. Nike released an advert starring Colin Kaepernick. After this commercial film got reaction of President D. Trump, a boycott campaign was initiated by dissentient consumers on social media with the hashtag #BurnYourNikes (Manfredi and Sancahez, 2019: 347). However, although the boycott created a negative interaction on Twitter, brand awareness increased while at the same time brand sales increased by 17% compared to last year due to the negative reaction of D. Trump (Cosentino, 2019, p. 61; NBS News, 2018).

In this context, Nike's support to the George Floyd Protests, which is also in the field of political activism in some ways; increased with their statement that they would support African American citizens with 40 million dollars in the next 4 years to fight against racism (Patel, 2020). Therefore, it is seen that the brand is engaged in "authentic" activism with its ties to the black community, its high level of activist message strategy and its reflection of anti-discrimination philosophy in the field of corporate behavior.

Legal Activism	Analysis
Walmart-ABD  *To best serve our communities and protect the health and safety of our shoppers and associates, face coverings will be required in all stores beginning Monday, July 20. For more on our decision and policy, please see here:* https://bit.ly/3h34FNK *NRF calls on retailers to set nationwide mask policy.* http://ow.ly/roKn50Az7Jl	Walmart has published a regulation requiring the wearing of a mask in order to protect public health in the Covid-19 epidemic affecting the whole world (Sarkar & Kotler, 2020). The main reasons for this regulation to be legal activism include the fact that the company focuses on the working environment and the health of its employees, and also the discussions on wearing masks are fierce in the public. In the USA, the anti-mask statements of President D. Trump in the first period of the epidemic, but his encouragement for the putting mask on in the following process and the different views of the citizens made the matter of mandatory mask wearing a controversial and political issue (Yan, 2020; Reynolds, 2020). In the Covid-19 outbreak, Walmart was recognized by the National Retail Federation, of which it is a member, for its successful leadership in the pandemic process. National Retail Federation made a call to all retailers in the USA about supporting a law that requires the use of masks for customers who go shopping during the pandemic; while also they proposed to the White House in partnership with other trade organizations to enact a law mandating the use of masks in public places (Sarkar & Kotler, 2020). In this context, it is seen that Walmart supports legal activism actions on public / employee health through its trade organizations. However, Walmart has been criticized for providing the lowest hourly wage and insufficient family assistance in the US for its employees and not meeting the health insurance of part-time employees (Hyman, 2018; Hines, 2012). In this sense, the "legal activity" support given by Walmart to protect the health of the society and its employees is baseless, due to the fact that the company does not provide its personnel with adequate health insurance and comfortable working conditions

CONSUMER

	in practice. Therefore, it is seen that Wallmart has implemented "inauthentic" brand activism implementations.
Political Activism	**Analysis**
1. Ben and Jerry's-ABD 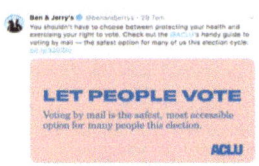 *You shouldn't have to choose between protecting your health and exercising your right to vote. Check out the @ ACLU's handy guide to voting by mail - the safest option for many of us this election cycle: LET PEOPLE VOTE Voting by mail is the safest, most accessible option for many people this election.* https://twitter.com/benandjerrys/status/1288520107069767680	Ben & Jerry's has launched a political campaign to encourage citizens to vote in the US Presidential election in November 2020, in collaboration with the ACLU, which acts to protect the constitution and laws as well as individual rights and freedoms in the US. The campaign, which wants to encourage people to vote by mail, with the thought that voting will be limited due to the Covid-19 epidemic, is an example of political activism. The main reason why this announcement made on Twitter has the characteristics of political activism is that it aims to prevent people's voting and democratic rights from being interrupted by the pandemic. The main reason why the Mail voting practice is "controversial" in the USA in the presidential elections planned to take place in November 2020 is that the Republican Party and D. Trump claim that such an application across the country will not be healthy and may even be fraudulent. In addition, the requirement to be registered in the country to vote and concerns about possible confusion in the postal system also fuel the debate on implementation. In contrast, Democrats support facilitating voter access, including postal voting, to encourage election participation (Parks, 2020; Ewings, 2020). In this context, while postal voting debate has become a growing topic of discussion between Republicans and Democrats; businesses can also give a "progressive" response to these discussions, as seen in the example of Ben & Jerry's. Ben & Jerry's has been conducting social campaigns that will be a catalyst for social change since the 1980s. In addition, "democracy" is among the core values of Ben & Jerry's; there are informative and social movement studies in different political areas such as freedom of vote, local elections, voting by mail (Ben & Jerry's, 2020). In this sense, this campaign that is carried out in connection with the issue of voting by mail, which is in a "controversial" position in the country, strengthens the "authentic" and activist brand personality.
Environmental Activism	**Analysis**
1. Patagonia-ABD  *The US Forest Service is moving forward with plans to open up the Tongass National Forest to development. Join the Southeast Alaska Conservation Council webinar on Tuesday, May 12 and learn how you can take action to protect the Tongass.*	Patagonia has been working as an environmentally friendly brand since the 2000s; this strategy is based on fundamental values such as producing the best product, not harming the environment, and being eco-friendly. Also, the brand describes itself as an activist (Clement, 2020, Patagonia, 2020). Patagonia invites activists to an informative seminar on the action plan to protect Tongass in its Twitter post against the plan to open the Tongass National Forest for development which is shared by The US Forest Service. This sharing is based on a high activist message strategy and is included in the "authentic brand activism" activities as it aims to create awareness and hence reaction to environmental problems. In addition, by putting the environmental protection value of Patagonia in the center, mediating an activity that requires high participation in organizational practice and framing the problems of the society by producing solutions; it is seen that they have the aim of being pro-open society brand. The main reasons why Tongass National Forest's opening to commercial operation is highly controversial is that it has been guaranteed by federal law since 2001, the Trump's administration wants to open the region to timber trade and road construction despite the fact that it is one of the largest forests in the country, and hence it matters for combating climate change. Due to its importance, environmental activist groups strongly oppose this bill. However, those who defend the bill have an economic argument for the

Business Activism	Analysis
	development of Alaska; also claim that natural life will be protected as well (Kwong, 2019). Patagonia, on the other hand, has made a call for environmentalist formations and citizens to activism via Twitter, as the protection of natural habitats and forests is among its main fields of activity regarding this social conflict issue.
1. Unilever-ABD *Half of all managerial roles across Unilever are now represented by women. Here are nine ways we have created a more balanced business: http://bit.ly/32Pdvsy #GenderBalance #IWD2020* https://twitter.com/Unilever 	Unilever, in its work initiated to ensure gender equality in the workplace because it observes the balanced distribution of the genders of its personnel working at management levels; therefore, this Twitter post is under the business activism category. This problem, which is defined as the "gender gap" that Unilever tries to solve in business life, means the obstacles to the rise of women in business life and their earning in lower wages than their male colleagues. Although the hourly income of women in the USA varies according to variables such as race and socio-economic capital, it is lower than male workers. (avg. hourly wage: $ 1 male, $ 0.82 female) (AAUW, 2019). In addition, in the "glass ceiling" index ranking, which is named as the invisible barrier for women to gain high positions in business life, USA ranked 20th in 2018; values such as representation and salary, union affiliations, market access in jobs that require expertise are analyzed (Economist, 2019). The development of Unilever gender balance policy started in 2009 and runs the "Unstereotype Alliance" created by UN Women. Unilever received the 2020 Catalyst Award for promoting women's development and equality in business. In addition, the diversity & inclusion strategy of the enterprise includes strengthening the participation of women in the management and protecting the personnel from stereotypes in the work environment (Unilever, 2020a, Unilever, 2020b). In this context, Unilever, acting with the mission of gender equality in the workplace, because it places basic human values such as equality and inclusiveness among "prosocial values" and puts "gender balance" policy into practice; it seems that the brand activism form is "authentic". Unilever's effort to be among the leading brands in breaking down the masculine structure in the business world is another factor that strengthens the activist brand identity.
2. Eczacıbaşı Turkey  *"We started the degendered resume application for the first time in Turkey. The application ensures equal*	Eczacıbaşı Turkey tweeted a post in a similar way with Unilever by a "gender balance" focus. Shared campaign content aims to eliminate glass ceiling and gender gap problem in professional business life in Turkey. Turkey's glass ceiling index ranking was 27 in 2018 (The Economist, 2018). According to World Economic Forum Global Gender Gap 2019 results, Turkey is ranked at 136 in terms of access to economic employment opportunities for women's (World Economic Forum, 2019). These results reflects the gender inequality issue in business life of Turkey in detail. When Eczacıbaşı's related activities in women's social and business life are examined, it is seen that in 2012, they actively contributed to the Equality in Work Platform with the Ministry of Family and Social Policies. In 2012, the company successfully passed the audit conducted with KAGIDER and the

opportunities for candidates in the selection and placement process. Together with the gender-neutralized CV application, the CVs of the candidates who are at the interview stage are free from names, surnames, photographs, gender information, marital status, military service, family information and e-mail fields. " #Eczacıbaşı #togetherwe"	World Bank within the scope of the FEM (Equal Opportunity Model) initiative. In 2013, they signed the United Nations Women's Empowerment Principles (WEPs). In 2017, Eczacıbaşı Turkey launched its degendered resume application in order to ensure gender equality in business deals. Candidates who are in the selection and placement stage are evaluated without the fields of gender, name-surname, photograph, marital status, military service, family information and e-mail information. The equality of opportunity project called "together we" by Eczacıbaşı covers business processes from recruitment processes to leader training methods. The project, which was implemented on March 8, International Women's Day, aims to increase the female recruitment rate of white collar employees to 50%, the rate of white collar female employees to 40% and the rate of women in management to 35% by 2020 (Eczacıbaşı, 2020). Eczacıbaşı gives information about the gender-neutralized resume application in their Instagram post, which they shared with the motto "action speaks louder than gender". Similar to the campaign initiated by Unilever to increase the rate of women in businesses, the "togetherwe" project aims to raise awareness on this issue by focusing on basic human values such as equality and inclusion in the workplace. This study, which covers a long-term change process, can be evaluated in the context of "authentic brand activism." In addition, by combining the progressive style of the brand towards gender equality in business life with both an activist message strategy and workplace practices; it seems to transform it into a corporate philosophy.
Commercial Activism	**Analysis**
Ben& Jerry's -ABD	It is seen that Ben & Jerry's has a responsible behavior policy towards the working conditions of migrant workers from past to present. Having signed an agreement on this issue, the company aimed to ensure that migrant workers also have the right to pay amounting the standard in the state, as well as their leave and rest rights are adequate. Based on the Fair Food program, this agreement also encourages employees to speak out about violation of rights (Business and Human Rights Resource Center, 2017). Among the reasons why the immigration issue in the USA is a great "controversy", the draft law prepared by the D. Trump administration in 2018 to send immigrants out of the country by considering them illegal has an important place (Thomson, 2018). In addition, the unfairness of the working and living conditions of migrant workers places this matter among the controversial issues in the country. In their Twitter post, Ben & Jerry's retweeted the post shared by Fire Drill Fridays, which works to draw attention to climate change issues, and to point out the rights of daily workers who work without security. In the post shared by Ben & Jerry, they remark that immigrant workers should benefit from their basic worker rights regardless of their immigration status, and states that their health, safety and dignity should be protected. Ben & Jerry's displays a progressive attitude on this highly controversial issue in the society and gives its message with an activist approach. In addition, the brand's long-term protection of the rights of immigrant employees and realization of different practices together with signing of agreements show that it continues the authentic brand activism strategy with this sharing and aims to find solutions to the social problems experienced. In this sense, the effort of the brand to convey the importance it attaches to workers' rights to its brand value constitutes an example of "authentic brand activism".
Essential workers are risking their lives for our country. We must ensure that their health, safety, and dignity are protected by passing an Essential Worker Bill of Rights for all, regardless of immigration status. #ProtectEssentialWorkers #EWBOR https://twitter.com/benandjerrys/status/1258780874532945920	

Conclusion and Discussion

The fact that consumers expect brands to be sensitive towards social problems and solutions has caused some brands to take part in activist movements in accordance with their corporate culture, field of activity and management understanding. This strategy, defined as brand activism, enables consumers to see that brands consider social benefit; and it contributes positively to the image of brands in the long run. Brands take a stand on social and political issues and use brand activism as a marketing tactic in order to stand out in markets where competition is intense. Therefore, in this study, brand activism practices from examples of the Turkey and the United States are addressed, and activist messages given by brands on social media platforms have been analyzed from strategic and typological aspects.

CONSUMER

In the study, the examined samples were analyzed based on the classification of brand activism strategies of Kotler and Sarkar (2018, p. 632-636) and the brand activism typology of Vrendenburg et al. (2020: 6). In this research, social media posts of nine brands that can be considered in the context of brand activism were examined. In the category of social activism; Decathlon Turkey's combating against sexual orientation and Nike's struggle against race-based discrimination together with the Koç Holding's support for the Istanbul Convention for the elimination of violence against women is discussed. Daily life and work-life challenges faced by LGBT individuals, and violence against women as a social problem emerges in Turkey. The USA, on the other hand, has been the center of racial conflict and contention since its establishment. The traditional codes and historical background of both societies have laid the groundwork for these social problems. It has been observed that the messages shared by brands on social media platforms are carried out in order to draw attention to these problems and have the feature of autentic brand activism. Walmart's efforts to make the use of masks mandatory to protect public health in the Covid-19 process are considered as an example of legal activism. While this effort of Walmart, which exerts pressure on lawmakers regarding the use of masks, is evaluated in the context of legal activity; the fact that the company does not provide its personnel with sufficient health insurance and appropriate working conditions shows that Wallmart implements "inauthentic" brand activism practices.

The work initiated by Ben & Jerry's to encourage citizens to vote with confidence in the US Presidential elections in November 2020 has been evaluated in the context of political activism. This project, which aims to change the society, is included in the typology of "authentic brand activity" and strengthens the activist brand personality of them which comes from the past. Patagonia has been involved in environmental activism, with the content it shared against The US Forest Service's plan to open the Tongass National Forest to development. Patagonia, in accordance with its organizational mission, has mediated an activity that requires high participation, and has adopted an open society attitude by framing the problems of the society and generating solutions. In this respect, the activity has been evaluated within the typology of "authentic brand activity". In the context of commercial activism, the brands', Unilever in the US and Eczacıbaşı in Turkey, call for implementations has been determined to increase the level of representation of women in the work environment and the opportunity to create applications for equality. It has been concluded that these projects, which are carried out on the basis of inequality of opportunity in the business world, place basic human values such as equality and inclusiveness among "prosocial values" and apply the "gender balance" policy. Accordingly, it is seen that the typology of brand activism in implementations is "authentic". In the context of commercial activity, the content shared by the Ben & Jerry's brand on the rights of immigrant workers who work without security has been discussed. The brand has taken a progressive stance on precarious workers' rights, which is highly controversial in society, and has taken steps towards solving the problem. The brand's effort to convey the importance it attaches to workers' rights to its brand value has been evaluated within the "authentic brand activism" typology.

Considering the examples which were evaluated, it was seen that brands did not avoid activities that would affect social change and transformation, and they displayed a progressive attitude towards solving problems. However, in the study, despite the fact that the activism' activities carried out in Turkey were limited social and commercial activism practices, it was found that the different types of commercial practices have place in the US. In this case, although civil society in the US takes an active role in the solution of social problems in a way that takes businesses in as well, companies coming in the position of main catalyst for the process of Turkey's social change is still regarded as associated with being in the development stage. However, because these studies carried out on the basis of examples in brand' sharings as descriptive analysis, it does not contain generalizations on brand activism' activities of businesses in Turkey.

Following this study's results, the finding that social media sharings by different brands in Turkey and USA including a brand activism strategy shows, consumer demand for the operation of taking a stand on social issues, which is among the most important results of Edelman's (2018) Trust Barometer report, is tried to be fullfilled by different brands in Turkey and USA. Besides, in both countries, for the purpose of brand activism, active usage of social media by businesses and taking a guiding / action-oriented attitude of brands like Patagonia, Ben & Jerry's (USA) towards the followers on issues such as environment, employee rights and voting process, is in line with the increasing demands of the consumers from brands to actively engage in activism activities on social media which is identified in Sprout Social (2018) research. In the research, it is determined that businesses operating on a global scale, especially in the USA, adopt the "authentic" brand activism on different issues; brands are beginning to meet the expectations of consumers to both give activist messages and take action on different issues as mentioned in Edelman's (2020, p. 12-16) Trust Baramoter report. However, as it is seen in the Wallmart example; since the businesses that carry out inauthentic brand activism activities are far from activist values and corporate practices, Vrendenburg et al. (2020) emphasized that their works have the potential to damage brand identity in the long run by creating "woke washing".

Social media platforms are channels where activist movements become visible with the aim of finding solutions and drawing attention to the present social, economic, political problems and environmental issues which comes from past to present in Turkey and USA. It is possible to say that the posts on social media aim high participation and therefore increase the impact level of the project. The fact that brands present their efforts to frame the problems experienced in society and find solutions to them in social media with a high activist message strategy shows that they have a pro-social brand aim. For this reason, "authentic brand activity" activities have been identified in most of the analyzed samples. Although the socio-political structure in Turkey makes it difficult for brands to participate in activist movements, existing practices need to be carefully examined by academic circles and revealed what their role in social change is. Also, Dodd and Supa 2014; Korschun et al. As (2019) notes, when planning brand activism activities that are likely to alienate some consumers, as Mukherjee and Althuizen (2018) discuss in their research, it is necessary to correctly analyze the beneficial and harmful aspects of brand activism for businesses. Thus, businesses that adress polarizing and controversial issues in society will be able to carry out the right strategic and tactical activities while demonstrating a "progressive" attitude both on social media and through corporate behavior.

REFERENCES

AAUW (2019). The Simple Truth About the Gender Gap. (Accessed June 27, 2020), Available at https://www.aauw.org/app/uploads/2020/02/Simple-Truth-Update-2019_v2-002

Al-Muslim, A. (2019). Gillette's Ad with a #MeToo Edge Gets Mixed Reactions, The Wall Street Journal (January 17). (Accessed June 11, 2020), Available at https://www.wsj.com/articles/gillettes-ad-with-a-metoo-edge-gets-mixed-reactions-11547754187

Alhouti, S., Johnson, C. M. & Holloway, B. B. (2016). Corporate Social Responsibility Authenticity: Investigating its Antecedents and

Outcomes. Journal of Business Research, 69 (3), 1242–49.

Anadolu Ajansı (2020). Tartışmaların odağındaki 'İstanbul Sözleşmesi'. (Accessed June 27, 2020), Available at https://www.aa.com.tr/tr/turkiye/tartismalarin-odagindaki-istanbul-sozlesmesi/1924988

Ben & Jerry's (2020). Values-Issues. (Accessed June 21, 2020), Available at https://www.benjerry.com/values/issues-we-care-about/democracy

Barton, R. et al. (2018), "To Affinity and Beyond: From Me to We, The Rise of the Purpose-led Brand," Accenture Strategy (December 5)..

Beise-Zee, R. (2013). Cause-Related Marketing, in Idowu, S.O., Capaldi, N., Zu, L., & Das Gupta, A. (eds), Encyclopedia of Corporate Social Responsibility. Berlin: Springer Verlag, pp. 321-326.

Bruder. C & Lubeck, H. (2019). It's Time To Become Brave - The Phenomenon of Social Brand Activism. Student Project. https://lup.lub.lu.se/student-papers/search/publication/8983571

Bocken, N. MP, Short, S. W., Rana, P. & Evans, S. (2014). A Literature and Practice Review to Develop Sustainable Business Model Archetypes. Journal of Cleaner Production, 65 (2014), 42–56.

Boren, C. (2018). "Nike's Colin Kaepernick Ad Campaign Gets More Yeas than Nays from Young People," The Washington Post. (Accessed 17, 2020) Available at https://www.washingtonpost.com/news/early-lead/wp/2018/09/13/colin-kaepernicks-nike-ad-campaign-gets-more-yeahs-than-nays-from-young-people/

Business &Human Rights Center (2017). USA: Ben & Jerry's and Migrant Justice reach agreement to improve migrant dairy workers' conditions. (Accessed June 27, 2020), Available at https://www.business-humanrights.org/en/latest-news/migrant-justice-and-ben-jerrys-reach.

Büyüköztürk, Ş. vd. (2018). Bilimsel Araştırma Yöntemleri, Ankara: Pegem Akademi, 2018, s.92-93.

Carrega, C.; Lloyd, Whitney (June 3, 2020). "Charges against former Minneapolis police officers involved in George Floyd's death". ABC News. (Accessed 17, 2020) Available at https://abcnews.go.com/US/charges-minneapolis-police-officers-involved-george-floyds-death/story?id=71045487

The Case for Cause Marketing - Statistics for Businesses & Nonprofits. (2018). (Accessed 17, 2020) Available at https://causegood.com/blog/cause-marketing-statistics/

Chatterji, A. K. & Toffel, M. W. (2018). The New CEO Activists, Harvard Business Review (January - February).

Clement, M. (2020). Patagonia Brand Manifests Success Through Environmental Activism. Accessed 17, 2020) Available at https://www.nxtbookmedia.com/blog/patagonia-manifests-brand-success-through-environmental-activism/

Council of Europe (2020). Chart of signatures and ratifications of Treaty 210. (Accessed June 25, 2020), Available at https://www.coe.int/en/web/conventions/full-list/-/conventions/treaty/210/signatures

Cohn, E. (2017). We Are All Immigrants': Execs Speak out against Trump's Immigration Ban. Business Insider (January 30). (Accessed June 25, 2020), Available at https://www.greenwichtime.com/technology/businessinsider/article/WE-ARE-ALL-IMMIGRANTS-Execs-are-speaking-out-10894305.php

Cone Communications Research Confirms Millennials as America's Most Ardent CSR Supporters. (2015, September 23). (Accessed June 27, 2020), Available at http://www.conecomm.com/news-blog/newcone-communications-research-confirms-millennials-as-americas-most-ardent-csr-supporters

Cosentino, A. (2019). Risk and Reward: An Analysis of #BoycottNike as a Response o Nike's Colin Kaepernick Advertising Campaign. Elon Journal of Undergraduate Research in Communications. 10 (1):54-63.

Creswell, J. & Abrams, R. (2017). Shopping Becomes a Political Act in the Trump Era. New York Times (February 10). New York Times, (Accessed June 25, 2020), Available at nytimes.com/2017/02/10/business/

nordstrom-trump.html

Crimmins, J. & Horn, M. (1996). Sponsorship: From Management Ego Trip to Marketing Success. Journal of Advertising Research, 36 (4), 11–22.

Cutler, B. D. & Muehling, D. (1988). Advocacy Advertising and the Boundaries of Commercial Speech. Journal of Advertising. 18 (3).

Delmas, M. A. & Burbano, V. C. (2011). The Drivers of Greenwashing. California Management Review, 54 (1), 64–87.

Dey, I. (1993). Qualitative Data Analysis: A User-Friendly Guide for Social Scientists. London: Routledge Publications.

Dodd, M. D. & Supa, D. W. (2014). Conceptualizing and Measuring 'Corporate Social Advocacy' Communication: Examining the Impact on Corporate Financial Performance. Public Relations Journal, 8 (3), 1–23.

Dondurucu, Z.B. (2018). Eşcinsellik Temelli Nefret Söylemi İçeren İletilerin Twitter'da İncelenmesi. Erciyes İletişim Dergisi. 5(4): 513-534.

Drumwright, M. E. (1996). Company Advertising with a Social Dimension: The Role of Noneconomic Criteria. Journal of Marketing. 60(4). doi:10.2307/1251902

Du, S., Bhattacharya, C. B. & Sen, S. (2010). Maximizing Business Returns to Corporate Social Responsibility (CSR): The Role of CSR Communication. International Journal of Management Reviews, 12 (1): 8–19.

Economist (2018). Glass Ceiling Index. (accessed June 14, 2020), Available at https://www.economist.com/graphic-detail/2018/02/15/the-glass-ceiling-index

Economist (2019). Glass Ceiling Index. (Accessed June 17, 2020), Available at https://www.economist.com/graphic-detail/2019/03/08/the-glass-ceiling-index

Eczacıbaşı (2020). Aynası İştir Kişinin Cinsiyete Bakılmaz. (Accessed June 17, 2020), Available at https://www.eczacibasi.com.tr/tr/basin-odasi/

haberler/aynasi-istir-kisinin-cinsiyetine-bakilmaz.

Edelman (2018a). 2018 Edelman Trust Barometer Global Report. Research Report, Edelman Trust Barometer Annual Global Study. (accessed June 21, 2020), Available at https://www.edelman.com/sites/g/files/aatuss191/files/2018 10/2018_Edelman_Trust_Barometer_Global_Report_FEB.pdf

Edelman (2018b). 2018 Edelman Trust Barometer: Expectations for CEOs. Research Report, Edelman Trust Barometer Annual Global Study. (accessed June 21, 2020), Available at https://www.edelman.com/sites/g/files/aatuss191/files/2018-10/Edelman_Trust_Barometer_Implications_for_CEOs_2018.pdf.

Edelman (2018c). 2018 Edelman Earned Brand: Brands Take a Stand. Research Report, Edelman Trust Barometer Annual Global Study. (accessed June 15, 2020). Available at https://www.edelman.com/sites/g/files/aatuss191/files/2018-10/2018_Edelman_Earned_Brand_Global_Report.pdf

Edelman (2020). Brands and Racial Justice in America. Research Report, Edelman Trust Barometer Annual Global Study. (Accessed June 15, 2020). Available at https://www.edelman.com/sites/g/files/aatuss191/files/2018-10/2018_Edelman_Earned_Brand_Global_Report.pdf

Edgecliffe-Johnson, A. (2018). Dick's to Stop Selling Assault-style Rifles, CEO Calls for Gun Reform. Financial Times (March 1). (accessed June 15, 2020). Available at https://www.washingtonpost.com/business/economy/dicks-sporting-goods-overhauled-its-gun-policies.

Eisenberg, N. (1982). The Development of Prosocial Behavior. Cambridge: Academic Press.

Ewing, P. (2020). Voting And Elections Divide Republicans And Democrats Like Little Else. Here's Why. NPR. (Accessed June 15, 2020). Available at https://www.npr.org/2020/06/12/873878423/voting-and-elections-divide-republicans-and-democrats-like-little-else-heres-why

Flinders University (2019). Why Teach Controversial Issues? (Accessed June 29, 2020), Available at https://www.flinders.edu.au/teaching/quality/teaching-methods/teaching-controversial- issues/why-teach-controversial-issues.cfm.

Fox, K. FA (1986). The Measurement of Issue/Advocacy Advertising Effects. Current Issues and Research in Advertising, 9 (1-2), 61–92.

Gillette (2019). #TheBestMenCanBe," (January 15), (Accessed June 25, 2020), Available at https://gillette.com/en-us/about/the-best-men-can-be.

Gilliland, N. (2018). Five brand campaigns that took a stand on social issues. (January, 4). (Accessed June 29, 2020), Available at https://econsultancy.com/five-brand-campaigns-that-took-a-stand-on-social-issues/

Gray, A. (2019). "Brands Take a Stand for Good: The Effect of Brand Activism on Social Media Engagement". Master Thesis. University of New Hampshire. Durham.

Haley, E. (1996), Exploring the Construct of Organization as Source: Consumers' Understandings of Organizational Sponsorship of Advocacy Advertising. Journal of Advertising, 25 (2), 19–35.

Hines, A. (2012). Walmart's New Health Care Policy Shifts Burden To Medicaid, Obamacare. Huffington Post. (Accessed June 11, 2020). Available at https://www.huffpost.com/entry/walmart-health-care-policy-medicaid-obamacare_n_2220152.

Holder, A. (2017). Sex Doesn't Sell Any More, Activism Does. And Don't the Big Brands Know It. The Guardian (February 3). Accessed June 11, 2020). Available at https://www.theguardian.com/commentisfree/2017/feb/03/activism-sells-brands-social-conscience-advertising

Holt, D. B. (2002). Why Do Brands Cause Trouble? A Dialectical Theory of Consumer Culture and Branding. Journal of Consumer Research, 29 (1), 70–90.

Hoppner, J. J. & Vadakkepatt, G. G. (2019). Examining Moral Authority in the Marketplace: A Conceptualization and Framework. Journal of Business Research, 95, 417–27.

Hynman, J. (2018). Walmart (Yes, Walmart) Has Now Done More for Worker Rights Than the U.S. Government. Workforce. (Accessed June 13, 2020). Available at https://www.workforce.com/news/walmart-yes-walmart-now-done-worker-rights-u-s-government,

Ilga Europe (2020). Annual Review of the Human Rights Situation of Lesbian, Gay, Bisexual, Trans and Intersex People In Europe And Central Asia 2020. (Accessed June 13, 2020). Available at https://www.ilgaeurope.org/sites/default/files/Annual%20Review%202020.pdf

Inoue, Y. & Kent, A. (2014). A Conceptual Framework for Understanding the Effects of Corporate Social Marketing on Consumer Behavior. Journal of Business Ethics, 121 (4), 621–33.

Keys, T. Malnight, T.W. & van der Graaf, K. (2009). Making the most of corporate social responsibility. McKinsey Quarterly. pp. 1-8

Koç Sistem (2020). Kurumsal Sosyal Sorumluluk. (Accessed June 27, 2020), Available at https://www.kocsistem.com.tr/kurumsal/kurumsal-sorumluluk/kurumsal-sosyal-sorumluluk/

Korschun, D., Rafieian, H., Aggarwal, A. & Swain, S.D. (2019), Taking a Stand: Consumer Responses When Companies Get (or Don't Get) Political (July 3). (Accessed June 13, 2020). Available at SSRN: https://ssrn.com/abstract1/42806476 or http://dx.doi.org/10.2139/ ssrn.2806476.

Kotler, P. & Lee, N. (2005). Best of Breed: When it Comes to Gaining a Market Edge While Supporting a Social Cause, "Corporate Social Marketing" Leads the Pack. Social Marketing Quarterly, 11 (3-4), 91–103.

Kotler, P., & Lee, N. (2008). Kurumsal Sosyal Sorumluluk. İstanbul: MediaCat Yayınları.

Kotler, P. &, C. (2017), Finally, Brand Activism!" The Marketing Journal (January 9). (Accessed June 13, 2020). Available at http://www.marketingjournal.org/finally-brand-activism-philip -kotler-and-chris tian-sarkar/.

Kotler, P., Hessekiel, D. & Lee, N. (2012). Good Works!: Marketing and Corporate Initiatives that Build a Better World . . . and the Bottom Line. Hoboken, NJ: John Wiley & Sons.

Kwong, E. (2019). For Many, Issue Of Logging In America's Largest National Forest Cuts Deep. NPR. (Accessed June 15, 2020). Available at https://www.npr.org/2019/10/08/768251735/for-many-issue-of-logging-in-americas-largest-national-forest-cuts-deep,

Lee, M. & Yoon, H. J. (2020). When Brand Activism Advertising Campaign Goes Viral: An Analysis of Always #LikeAGirl Video Networks on YouTube. International Journal of Advanced Culture Technology. 8 (2).146-158.

Manfredi-Sánchez, J. L. (2019). Brand activism. Communication &Society, 32(4), 343-359.

Marzilli, T. (2017). Brands and politics: Spotlight on Starbucks. (Accessed June 13, 2020). Available at YouGov BrandIndex website https://www.brandindex.com/article/brands-and-politics-spotlight-on-starbucks.

Menon, S. & Kahn, B. E. (2003). Corporate Sponsorships of Philanthropic Activities: When Do They Impact Perception of Sponsor Brand?. Journal of Consumer Psychology, 13 (3), 316–27.

McKinsey & Company. (2009). Making the most of corporate social responsibility. (Accessed June 5, 2020). Available at https://www.mckinsey.com/featured-insights/leadership/making-the-most-of-corporate-social-responsibility.

Miller, B. & Janas S. (2009). Community Stakeholder Responses to Advocacy Advertising, Journal of Advertising, 38:2, 37-52, DOI: 10.2753/JOA0091-3367380203

Moorman, C. (2018). Big Brands And Political Activism: What Do Marketers Think?. Forbes. (September, 4) (Accessed June 15, 2020). Available at. https://www.forbes.com/sites/christinemoorman.

Moorman, C. (2020). Brand Activism in a Political World, Journal of Public Policy and Marketing, 39 (4), https://doi.org/10.1177/0743915620945260.

Mukherjee, S. & Althuizen, N. (2018), "Brand Activism: Does Courting Controversy Help or Hurt a Brand?" International Journal of Research in Marketing (published online March 13), 1-17. DOI:10.1016/j.ijresmar.2020.02.008.

Nalick, M., Josefy, M., Zardkoohi, A., & Bierman, L. (2016). Corporate Sociopolitical Involvement: A Reflection of Whose Preferences?.

Academy of Management Perspectives, 30 (4), 384–403.

NBC News (2018). What boycott? Nike sales are up 31 percent since the Kaepernick campaign. . (Accessed June 27, 2020), Available at https://www.nbcnews.com/business/business-news/what-boycott-nike-sales-are-31-percent-kaepernick-campaign-n908251

Park, M. (2020). Why Is Voting By Mail (Suddenly) Controversial? Here's What You Need To Know. NPR. (Accessed June 27, 2020), Available at https://www.npr.org/2020/06/04/864899178/why-is-voting-by-mail-suddenly-controversial-heres-what-you-need-to-know

Patagonia (2020). Activism. . (Accessed June 27, 2020), Available at https:// www.patagonia.com/activism/

Patel, S. (2020). Brands Follow Antiracist Statements With Donations. What's Next? Wall Street Journal. (Accessed June 26, 2020), Available at https://www.wsj.com/articles/brands-follow-anti-racist-statements-with-donations-whats-next-11591437600,

Reynolds, E. (2020). The mask debate is still raging in the US, but much of the world has moved on. CNN. (Accessed June 25, 2020), Available at https://edition.cnn.com/2020/07/21/europe/masks-debate-us-europe-asia-intl/index.html

Sarkar, C. & Kotler, P. (2018). Brand Activism: From Purpose to Action. Idea Bite Press.

Sarkar, C. & Kotler, P. (2020). Will Business Save Democracy?. Activist Brands. (Accessed June 27, 2020), Available at http://www.activistbrands.com/will-business-save-democracy/.

Sethi, S. Prakash (1979), "Institutional/Image Advertising and Idea/Issue Advertising as Marketing Tools: Some Public Policy Issues," Journal of Marketing, 43 (1), 68–78.

Shetty, S. Nagendra B & K. Anand (2019). "Brand activism and millennials: an empirical investigation into the perception of millennials towards brand activism" December 2019. Problems and Perspectives in Management 17(4). DOI: 10.21511/ppm.17(4).2019.-162-175.

Smith, N. C. & Korschun, D. (2018). Finding the Middle Ground in a Politically Polarized World. MIT Sloan Management Review, 60 (1), 1–6.

Soler P P. & Jiménez, E. A. M. (2012). "Reflexión sobre el rigor científico en la investigación cualitativa". Estudios sobre el Mensaje Periodístico, 18, 879-888. http://www.doi.org/10.5209/rev_ESMP.2012.v18.40966

Sprout Social (2018), "#BrandsGetReal: Championing Change in the Age of Social Media," Research report, Sprout Social (January 9). (Accessed June 23, 2020), Available at https://sproutsocial.com/insights/data/championing-change-in-the-age-of-social-media/

Taylor, D. B. (June 2, 2020). "George Floyd Protests: A Timeline". The New York Times. (Accessed August 27, 2020), Available at https://www.nytimes.com/article/george-floyd-protests-timeline.html

Thompson, D. (2018). How Immigration Became So Controversial. Atlantic. (Accessed August 27, 2020), Available at https://www.theatlantic.com/politics/archive/2018/02/why-immigration-divides/552125/

Tony's Chocolonely (2020), "Living Income Model," (Accessed July 4, 2020), Available at https://tonyschocolonely.com/nl/en/living-income-model

The British Academy (2019), Principles for Purposeful Business: How to Deliver the Framework for the Future of the Corporation - An Agenda for Business in the 2020s and Beyond. London: The British Academy.

Unilever (2019a). "Unilever CEO Warns Advertisers That 'Woke-Washing' Threatens Industry Credibility," press release (June 19). (Accessed August 27, 2020), Available at https://www.marketingdive.com/news/unilever-ceo-woke-washing-is-infecting-the-ad-industry/557170/

Unilever (2019b),."Unilever's Purpose-Led Brands Outperform," press release (June 11). (Accessed August 26, 2020), Available at unilever.com/news/news-and-features/Feature-article/2019/brands-with-purpose-grow-and-here-is-the-proof.html

Unilever (2020a). "Unilever achieves gender balance across management globally". (Accessed August 25, 2020), Available at https://www.

unilever.com/news/press-releases/2020/unilever-achieves-gender-balance-across-management.

Unilever (2020b). "Advancing diversity & inclusion". (Accessed August 25, 2020), Available at https://www.unilever.com/sustainable-living/enhancing-livelihoods/opportunities-for-women/advancing-diversity-and-inclusion/

Varadarajan, P. R. & Menon, A. (1988). Cause-Related Marketing: A Coalignment of Marketing Strategy and Corporate Philanthropy. Journal of Marketing, 52 (3), 58–74.

Viken Tuason, C. V. & Hermansen, M.A. (2019). "Brand Activism in a New Power World" A Case Study of the Social Media Communications of Patagonia". Master Thesis, Denmark: Aolborg University.

Vredenburg, J., Spry,A., Kemper, J. & Kapitan, S. (2018). Brands Taking a Stand: Authentic Brand Activism or Woke Washing?. Journal of Public Policy& Marketing. Special Issue. 1-17.

World Economic Forum (2020). Global Gender Gap Report 2020. (Accessed August 27, 2020), Available at https://www.weforum.org/reports/gender-gap-2020-report-100-years-pay-equality

Wettstein, F. & Baur, D. (2016). Why Should We Care About Marriage Equality?: Political Advocacy as a Part of Corporate Responsibility. Journal of Business Ethics, 138 (2), 199–213.

WGSN Insider (2017), "The Rise of Brand Activism," WGSN Insider (January 12), (Accessed August 25, 2020), Available at https://www.wgsn.com/blogs/the-rise- of-brand-activism-wgsn/#.

Wherry, F. and Schor, J. (2015). The SAGE Encyclopedia Of Economics And Society. USA: SAGE Publications.

Wikipedia (2020). George Floyd Protests. (Accessed August 27, 2020), Available at https://en.wikipedia.org/wiki/George_Floyd_protests

Yan, H. (2020). Top health officials have changed their minds about face mask guidance -- but for good reason. CNN. (Accessed August 27,

2020), Available at https://edition.cnn.com/2020/07/19/health/face-masks-us-guidance/index.html,

Yıldırım, A. ve Şimşek, H. (2008). Sosyal Bilimlerde Nitel Araştırma Yöntemleri, Ankara: Seçkin Yayıncılık.

CHAPTER 2

SERVICE FAILURE AND SERVICE RECOVERY IN THE CONTEXT OF CUSTOMER RELATIONS AND COMMUNICATION

Derya Fatma BİÇER
Asst. Prof. Dr.
Sivas Cumhuriyet University, Faculty of Economics and Administrative Sciences, Department of Business Administration
dfbicer@cumhuriyet.edu.tr
orcid.org/0000-0002-3359-1236

Abstract

Due to their unique characteristics, services have a structure that the service provider and the customer frequently encounter and critical moments can be experienced in these encounters. Service errors that may occur for this reason and the necessary compensation practices for solving these errors are critical for businesses in today's competitive environment. The achievement of customer satisfaction and loyalty depends on the establishment of effective and correct communication with the customer and thus the establishment of permanent relations between the business and the customer. In this part of the book, service errors that may arise in service businesses in the context of customer relations and communication and methods of compensating these errors will be included.

Keywords: *Service Failure, Service Recovery, Customer Relations, Communication*

Introduction

The concept of service can be defined as action, activity or satisfaction, which can be expressed more abstractly than physical goods that meet the needs of consumers. Today, many factors such as technological developments, the increase in the number of educated individuals, the increase in the level of welfare, the increase in the population and the increase in the number of employed personnel, the complexity of life, the improvement of the life expectancy and consciousness of the consumers have enabled the service sector to develop gradually.

https://doi.org/10.2478/9788366675247-002

This prevalence has also led to the active presence of the service sector in the economy. Because of its unique characteristics, unlike physical goods, a number of failures may occur in the process of production and consumption of services caused by inside or outside the company. For this reason, recovering for these failures creates added value for companies at the point of ensuring customer satisfaction, achieving customer loyalty, performing positive word-of-mouth communication activities about the company and improving the quality of service by developing foresight while recovering for failures.

The service sector, which is one of the most important indicators of economic development, is an area where customer relations and communication also gain importance, especially as a result of the intense experience of the encounter moments of the service provider and receiver. Today, due to increasing competition and changing consumer profile, the trend of enterprises to differentiate in order to create customer value and customer-oriented perspective has gradually increased. Whether it's a manufacturing business or a service business, the business's touchpoints with its customers are retail or online service areas. In addition to acquiring, protecting, deepening new customers, creating satisfaction and loyalty, as well as developing strategies to prevent existing customers from shifting to competing businesses, has become an important and current concern of businesses. At this point, even production enterprises today define themselves as service enterprises in terms of the ability to produce on demand and the customer-oriented functionality of distribution channels.

In this section of the book, information about service failures that are likely to occur in service enterprises and recovery methods that enable customers to satisfy by eliminating these service failures, Customer Relationship Management and customer communication is given.

1. Service Concept

A service is an activity or benefit that one party offers to the other, which is basically untouchable and does not result in ownership of anything (Öztürk, 2009, p. 4). Service is also defined as actions that meet people's needs. Therefore, whether the service is carried out through individuals or technological means, it is all actions that ultimately have no physical presence and are aimed at meeting the needs of customers (Bayuk, 2006, p. 2). The abstraction, indivisibility, variability, instability, non-stockpiling of services, lack of life span, time dimension and offering according to demand make them different from physical products (Gümüş, 2012, p. 7-8).

The possibility of encounter and contact with the customer in the services is high. Contact with the customer is experienced face-to-face or through digital media, the level of contact may increase depending on the type of Service. These moments when communication and interaction occur are called critical moments, and positive or negative situations experienced at critical moments have a high impact on the level of quality that customers perceive from the service.

2. Service Failure

In today's conditions, especially labor-intensive service enterprises strive to produce and provide services that can provide customer satisfaction and meet customer expectations. Customers ' expectations are not fully met, or in some negative situations that occur during the design or presentation of the service, customer dissatisfaction occurs, as a result, the company may face customer loss (Zeithamel & Bitner, 2003, p. 181). This is referred to as a service failure.

As for service failure, it is possible to find various definitions in the literature. A service failure is a condition in which the product is insufficient to meet the customer's expectations due to a failure at any point in the service supply chain (Mueller et al., 2003, p. 1780). Service failure generally leads to a poor perception of the quality of the service at the stage of service delivery, and in this case, there is a need for personnel to perform appropriate correction operations (Shostack, 1984, p. 133).

Service failure is essentially that the service performance being offered is below customers ' expectations (Bell & Zemke, 1987, p. 32). In other words, a service failure occurs as a result of unusual situations in the product being provided to the customer and the process of obtaining this product, the environment in which the service is provided, the behavior of staff, or the behavior of other customers (Chua et al., 2010, p. 182). If it is necessary to summarize, service failure is the general name given to failures that occur outside of the activities planned by the company during the service in which customers are negatively affected during the marketing of the service (Parasuraman et al., 1991, p. 39). The service failure process is shown in Table 1 (Günaydın & Işık, 2017, p. 243).

Table 1: Service Failure Process

Stage 1	Customer service request,
Stage 2	Giving incomplete service to meet the demand
Stage 3	Providing deficient service in response to customer demand
Stage 4	Failure of the service provided to meet the demand
Stage 5	Perception of lack of service as a problem
Stage 6	Reporting the problem
Stage 7	Occurrence of service failure

As can be seen from the table, the service failure process is completed by identifying and accepting the negative situation resulting from the realization of an incomplete service provision in exchange for the customer's demand.

2.1. Types of Service Failure

Different types of failures arise depending on the area of activity of the service business and whether the level of encounter with customers is high. Service failure types are an issue that is extremely important for companies to perform a successful recovery process by identifying the recovery strategy/method that is compatible with the failure type (Swanson & Hsu, 2009, p. 188).

Bitner et al. (1990) according to service failures were evaluated in three categories:

i. Failures related to service delivery: Due to the loss of the booking record, the room or table booked cannot be served to the customer, the slowness in service delivery, the problems experienced on the plane or related to the flight, in the form of uncontrollable service failures.

ii. Failures related to employee behavior: These are service failures caused by rude and inappropriate behavior towards customers.

iii. Failures caused by not meeting special customer requests: Vegetarian menu request, etc. failures caused by failure to meet specific customer requests.

There are different approaches to the classification of service failures. According to Hoffman et al, three basic classifications can be mentioned.

These (Hoffman et al, 1995, p. 53):

i. Service failures caused by the service system: Service failures include failures caused by the base product.

ii. Service failures caused by non-fulfillment of customer requests: Includes service failures that occur from the point of customer requests for the service.

iii. Failures caused by the conduct of the staff: Includes failures caused by the unacceptable behavior of the staff or the primary responsibility of the staff.

Nguyen and McColl-Kennedy (2003) classify service failures as follows (Nguyen & McColl-Kennedy 2003, p. 50):

i. Result failures and process failures: The result is related to what customers perceive from the service, and the dissatisfaction of customers as a result of the service presented leads to the result failure. The process, on the other hand, is related to the service delivery time and is related to customer dissatisfaction during the service delivery.

ii. Failure size: It is related to the degree to which the service failure occurred is large or small in the eyes of customers.

iii. Self-and non-self-failures: Large failures that occur in the presentation together with the service constitute self-failures. Dissatisfaction, which is great in the eyes of customers, is self-failure, while failures in which dissatisfaction is small are expressed as non-self-failures.

2.2. Customer Responses to Service Failures

Customers who have encountered service failure experience unhappiness / dissatisfaction due to their negative experience and this negative experience negatively affects the customers' tendency to buy the same service again (Keaveney, 1995, p. 73).

Hirschman (1970) mentions that customers react actively or react passively as a result of a service failure. Here, the active response is related to the reaction of the customer; the passive response is stated as dissatisfaction, hesitation to complain together, and failure to act to complain. Landon (1977) mentions that as a result of a service failure, the customer can exhibit two types of behavior in the form of reacting or being unresponsive as a result of dissatisfaction.

McDougall & Levesque (1999) classified customer responses to service failures as follows:

i. Reaction: It is when customers pass their complaints to the service server.

ii. Negative word-of-mouth communication: When customers are dissatisfied, they pass this situation on to others.

iii. Leaving: The dissatisfied customer ends the relationship with the company.

iv. Loyalty: Customers continue to hope that everything in the company will be better in the future.

3. Service Recovery

In this section, the definition of service recovery, service recovery paradox, theories of service recovery, service recovery strategies, effective service recovery and service recovery results are discussed.

Service recovery is a process that is carried out in order to correct the service failure (Kwon & Jang, 2012, p. 1236). Service recovery is expressed as a planned and thought out process for the re-satisfaction of the victim customer when the product or service cannot meet the expectations of the customers (Zemke & Bell, 1990).

Service recovery is a process that covers all methods used to solve the current problem along with service failures that occur (Grönroos, 1990, p. 5). However, according to Schoefer (2008), it is possible to express service recovery as the activities implemented by the companies in order not to lose these customers if the customers are not satisfied with the service failures.

The main purpose of service recovery is to improve the pleasure/satisfaction level of the customer who has experienced service failure (Bitner et al., 1990, p. 71). In other words, service recovery is the actions taken by the firm against the failures related to the service and the purpose here is to continue the business relationship with the customers (Schweikhart et al., 1993).

According to Boshoff (1999), there are 6 dimensions of service recovery. These dimensions:

i. Communication: It is the dimension related to the fact that the personnel in charge of service delivery express their situation clearly, communicate with the customer through questions and answers to clarify the situation, and be understanding, reliable and honest.

ii. Empowerment: It is about the extent to which personnel receiving customer complaints can solve the problem and whether they can cope with the complaint without the help of any staff.

iii. Feedback: It is related to whether the firm provides feedback on the progress made during problem solving, as well as whether it apologizes in writing.

iv. Recovery / compensation: It is related to the apology for the financial loss suffered by the customer due to the service fault and the guarantee that he will not experience any financial loss.

v. Explanation: Whether the service provider made a detailed explanation of the failures, to what extent this explanation was satisfactory, how and why the problem arose, when it is not known, it is related to explanations that took place without responsibility and without apology.

vi. Tangible features: Whether the staff working in the service delivery is well dressed is related to working in a clean, orderly and professional environment.

3.1. The Service Recovery Paradox

Considering the importance of efforts to compensate for this failure after service failure, the concept of service recovery paradox has been introduced by McCollough & Bharadwaj (1992) in the field of service recovery. The service recovery paradox; It is the name given to the situation where the customers who are faced with a service failure, the problem is solved by the business with the service recovery and who are fully satisfied have more tendency to buy again compared to the customers who have not encountered any service failure in the first time (Lovelock & Wirtz, 2011). The service recovery paradox is when customers perceive high recovery performance, when the satisfaction level after service recovery is higher than the satisfaction before the service failure. Accordingly, it can be said that an effective service recovery results in higher satisfaction compared to a service that was provided without any failure at the first time (Matos et al., 2007, p. 60).

The satisfaction achieved within the framework of the service recovery paradox is the result of the company's responses to compensating for the service failure, and the satisfaction with the service recovery strategies it implements. Through the service recovery paradox, it is stated that the companies can regain their customers, the recycled customers will be more satisfied, and they can establish long-term and robust relationships with the company, and as a result, the service recovery costs of the firm may decrease (Vázquez et al., 2012, p. 86).

As part of the service recovery paradox, it may seem logical for companies to make a service failure to achieve greater satisfaction and then compensate for this failure, but this is essentially unrealistic. Because it is expensive to compensate for service failures, reliability is also an important element of service quality (Zeithamel & Bitner, 2003, p. 189). The possibility of a shake-up of customer confidence should also not be ignored when such a strategy is determined.

In fact, after effective service recovery, customers ' expectations increase and they expect the same excellent service recovery in response to future service failures in a standard way. In addition, after a second service failure, this situation disappears, and the service recovery Paradox also loses its existence (Lovelock & Wirtz, 2011).

3.2. Service Recovery Strategies

In today's conditions, many companies are aware of the need to create positive results by bringing their customers who have service failures and disappointments to the desired level of satisfaction. The positive results desired by companies can only be achieved through the effective implementation of service recovery. In this regard, when the service failures perceived by the customers reach the company through complaints, the attempts made by the companies are expressed as service recovery strategies (Grönroos, 1988).

The most widely accepted approach to how service failure should be compensated is the 5 methods put forward by Bell & Zemke (1987) :

i. Apologizing: Apologizing is like a blinding glance to a clearly visible failure, and failure recovery requires absolute acceptance of the failure by the firm as soon as the failure occurs. Without acknowledging the failure, there can be no remedy. Apologies are more effective when it comes from the person taking the responsibility as an authority.

ii. Immediate recovery: It is very important to immediately restore the situation caused by the disruption in service and correct the failure. Even if it is not possible to restore it in some cases, the sincere and serious initiatives of the service provider may be sufficient to satisfy the customer and even if the failure in the service cannot be corrected, the problem may disappear for the customer. If the customer is only angry and does not feel victim yet, urgent recovery efforts with apology may be sufficient to return the customer to normal.

iii. Empathy: Showing affection is the basic element of service delivery. Empathy is the application of the view that" you are not competent to change my feelings and my view until you show that you understand what I feel and my point of view." Thanks to empathy, the client can feel that he is taken care of, understood, heard, and accepted the misfortune that has happened to him. Solving the problem without addressing the feelings of a person experiencing a service failure is not enough to normalize the situation, and since the frustration experienced by the person remains constant, the state of dissatisfaction also continues. Therefore, in an effective service failure management, it is necessary that customers ' feelings are not forgotten.

iv. Symbolic atonement: It is the reinforcement of saying" We want to make up for the situation " by using a symbol. This symbol is a free drink, a gift voucher, etc. it could be gifts.

v. Following the process: This method is especially applicable in situations where the customer feels victim. It is possible to get a feedback from the customer by following the situation after the service failure. The positive results obtained when the process is followed also increases the self-confidence of the personnel who made the service mistake.

Bell & Zemke (1987) 5, which is introduced by methodically strategy together with the bell and Ridge (1992) "don't apologize", "the transaction is corrected and re-done" and "additional recovery/gift presenting in the form of" 3 method; McDougall and Levesque (1999) by "apology," "help," and "recovery" in the form of 3 method; Bitner et al. (1990) 4 methods in the form of "knowing where the failure was made", " revealing the reasons for this service failure", "apologizing at the right time" and "providing recovery such as free tickets, food, drinks" ; Boshoff (1997) also recommended 3 methods: "a senior official within the company should react quickly to the failure", "refund of all customer losses, as well as providing additional recovery", and "a senior manager should provide a large amount of recovery".

3.3. Effective Service Recovery

The fact that the human factor is a very important factor in service enterprises as a result of being both service provider and buyer, and that the failures cannot be completely eliminated due to the unique characteristics of services enabled the researchers to focus on methods that aim to eliminate the negative effects of these failures effective service recovery service on the satisfaction of customers (Arrow et al. , 2007, p. 3).

Lovelock & Wirtz (2011) state that effective service recovery has five basic rules listed below:

i. Service recovery should be proactive: An ideally appropriate return should be initiated before the customer has a chance to complain. It is important that service personnel are sensitive to signs of dissatisfaction and ask if the customer is experiencing a problem.

ii. Planning the procedures for service recovery: It is necessary to develop emergency plans for service failures that may occur regularly and are outside the system.

iii. Having taught service recovery skills: When service failures occur, staff may feel insecure and have to consult another staff member for help. However, if the staff help each other, some problems may arise. In this regard, it is an important issue to train the personnel for service failures and to teach them what to do in case of failure.

iv. Service recovery requires authorized personnel: Efforts for service recovery need to be flexible and staff must gain the power to use judicial and communication skills to develop solutions that satisfy complaining customers. This is especially true for unusual failures that are not caused by companies themselves, but which still require potential solutions.

Effective service recovery is the process of addressing customer complaints and creating positive customer responses. However, according to Ennew and Schoefer (2003), effective responses to customer complaints are very important in terms of satisfaction, the tendency to buy again, and word-of-mouth communication. In addition, Kelley & Davis (1994) emphasize that effective service recovery will lead to a higher perception of the quality of the products and services that customers buy, and even the image of the company will be positively affected.

It is possible to list the important benefits that successful service recovery activities can provide as follows (Lewis, McCann, 2004, p. 7):

- To improve the perceptions of consumers,
- To provide service and organization quality,
- Leading to positive word of mouth marketing,
- To increase consumer satisfaction,
- To build consumer relationships based on loyalty and have a positive impact on profits.

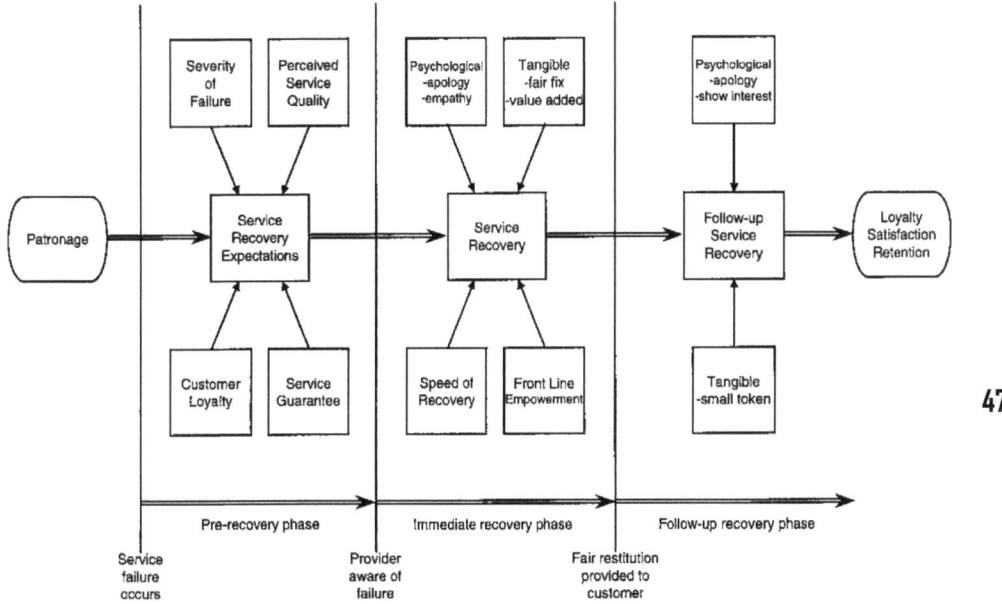

Figure 1: *Service Recovery Model (Miller et al., 2000, p. 388).*

In addition, compensating for service failures has various short-term and long-term consequences. Short-term results and satisfaction or dissatisfaction shows itself as basically to complain, while long-term results are mainly positive or negative word-of-mouth communication and loyalty to the enterprise or the operator drop-shaped (Eren, 2015, p. 608-609).

Therefore, since both short and long term customer dissatisfaction and the accompanying loss of customers are situations that businesses do not want at all, developing a sincere, permanent and systematic relationship with the customer is essential to anticipate existing and potential failures.

4. Customer Relations Management

With the decrease in the effectiveness of mass media, there has been a dramatic change in the way customers communicate with each other and with businesses. Marketing communication has also evolved from mass media to directed environments and based on interaction. At this point, relational marketing and establishing and maintaining permanent customer relationships have become one of the surest ways to create sustainable competitive advantage in most sectors (Clark & Melancon, 2013, p. 132).

Customer-centered management philosophy should be one of the main principles in the organization in order to develop business processes suitable for today's changing consumer profile and to understand the customer in the long term. Customer relationship management (CRM) strategies have become increasingly important worldwide, due to changes in customer expectations as well as changes in the structure of markets. As a result of a comprehensive study, CRM benefits can be summarized as follows, according to the recent CRM studies (Keith et al., 2008; Catalán-Matamoros, 2012, p. 2):

i. Developing the ability to target profitable customers,
ii. Integrated offerings across channels,
iii. Increased sales force efficiency and effectiveness,
iv. Personalized marketing messages,
v. Customized products and services,
vi. Improving customer service efficiency and effectiveness,
vii. Improved pricing.

Customer Relationship Management (CRM) is a combination of people, processes, and technology that firms support when trying to understand their customers. CRM, an integrated approach to managing and developing relationships established by focusing on customer retention and relationship with the customer, has essentially evolved from developments in Information Technology and organizational changes in customer-oriented processes. In addition, defining processes and roles in the firm also allows managers to identify dynamics that concern all business functions, including communication flows and models of inter-unit coordination (Catalán-Matamoros, 2012, p. 3-4).

For this reason, CRM is a powerful concept in both managerial and marketing axes that should be used by all companies that want to achieve competitive advantage by creating customer value in today's business world, and especially by service businesses where face-to-face contact with the customer is effective. The most powerful marketing communication instrument in service businesses is undoubtedly word-of-mouth communication. Customer relationship management is of great importance in making word-of-mouth communication a positive and continuous marketing tool, and creating long-term relationships that can be used to anticipate potential service failures or develop service recovery strategies.

4.1. Customer Orientation

CRM literature emphasizes the importance of developing customer orientation in all units within the company. Customer focus within the CRM system allows the firm to support marketing campaign efficiency and meet customer needs by exploring them. Therefore, customer orientation, CRM system to help solve customer problems as customer satisfaction to perform marketing activities, especially to manage the needs of existing customers helps to identify possible alternatives and customer satisfaction will continue to increase easily. Therefore, customer focus directly leads to customer-centric information quality and contributes to company performance (Garrido-Moreno & Padilla - Meléndez, 2011, p. 437).

A customer-centered organizational system allows the firm to devote itself to customer-centered actions such as initiating customer information sharing, developing customer relationships, and deepening. Successful implementation of CRM projects requires companies to be customer-oriented in addition, it guides the organization's attitude towards implementing CRM activities, which puts more emphasis on launching and maintaining long-term customer relationships.

Businesses need to strengthen their customer-focused strategies to improve and successfully execute customer relationship management. Because at the moment today, customized marketing campaigns or one-to-one marketing campaigns refer to campaigns and communications that contain marketing messages tailored to a specific customer, their specific profile, preferences and needs. In the past, to achieve maximum customer numbers and economies of scale, firms used collective marketing and targeted the entire market. But as marketing moved from product-centric to customer-centric, marketers began to use campaign-based marketing and target specific segmented customer groups. Today, customized marketing is expected to be the next widespread marketing trend, promising firms to gain competitiveness through differentiation in an increasingly competitive market. It is also very important that marketing managers are aware of this rising trend when creating CRM strategies for the company (Kumar & Petersen, 2017, p. 227).

4.2. Customer Relations and Communication

In order to move the value of the relationship established with the customer to the highest point, CRM is an important process in which activities that initiate, maintain and terminate the relationship in all areas of encounter are carried out and directed (Reinartz et al., 2004, p. 63). In CRM, the relationship between customer and business is to increase customer value and therefore customer satisfaction, and as a result, create loyalty and become a reason for choice again. CRM system is an innovative technology designed to manage customer relationships (Chen & Popovich, 2003; Chang, Park & Chaiy, 2010). This system is widely used to collect, integrate and analyze customer information (such as information from a salesperson's interactions with customers). In addition to the correct processing of customer information, the quality of customer information is also very important for CRM performance. Here, quality means the integration, timeliness and usefulness of customer information into processes (Mueller & Nyfeler, 2011; Chuang & Lin, 2013, p. 271).

CRM is essentially a philosophy of a business as a whole that concerns stakeholders and requires a long-term system, and business management is a customer-oriented approach, so the marketing unit should work together. According to these explanations, CRM is a new concept in the field of relationship-based marketing, but the underlying idea is not new, but very simple; it refers to the "one-on-one marketing" strategy, which means treating different customers differently. The basic mechanism of this strategy involves understanding how customers differ and creating a strategy for how the firm should behave according to each customer due to these differences (Crimea, 2001, p. 47-49).

What needs to be done here is to focus and invest in establishing meaningful and lasting relationships with the customer. Relationship investment means the investment made for the resources focused on establishing a stronger relationship together with the time and labor costs of the enterprise (Palmatier, Dant, Grewal, & Evans, 2006, p. 138). Businesses should carry out this process with an organizational culture that considers the needs of customers to be prioritized, an organization system that encourages customer relationships, and information technology that provides customer information acquisition and analysis (Whang & Feng, 2012, p. 118).

However, in order to plan customer relationships correctly, the organization as a whole must be able to quickly and accurately access customer information and use this information in the most appropriate way. A lot of work falls on the employees here. If employees do not share useful, timely, or accurate customer information, neither the firm nor customers will receive any benefit.

The use of CRM systems is likely to affect the quality of customer information. For example, CRM systems can improve the integration of customer information, such as combining customer transaction data with data from other sources or combining customer information from different touchpoints (Boulding, Staelin, Ehret, & Johnston, 2005, p. 156-157; Payne & Frow, 2005, p. 68). CRM systems can help provide fast and unique front office support or conduct marketing operations more efficiently by increasing the timeliness of customer information (Chen & Popovich, 2003).

CRM, işletmelerin müşterilerle ilişkilerini düzenleyen ve sürdüren, yöntemleri, yazılımları ve tüm çevrimiçi süreçleri içeren ve bilgi endüstrisinde var olan bir kavramdır (Xu et al., 2002, p. 447). In other words, multiple channels such as CRM applications, face-to-face encounters in customer communication, telephone and Web page visits are combined. In this way, it allows customers and businesses to communicate in convenient and flexible ways. CRM also helps businesses to deepen their customers in an approach that complements each other with relative marketing. What is valid in relationship marketing is that all departments within the business work in harmony and thus bring profitability to the business (Grönroos, 1991; Gülmez & Bookseller, 2003, p. 82).

4.3. Customer Information Systems and CRM Technology

Today, businesses need to use the concept of business intelligence as a strategic advantage in order to cope with global competition. In order to properly adapt this concept to business, it is necessary to use information and communication technologies and electronic networks in order to have modern business information systems and to make processes effective (Habul et al., 2012, p. 16).

CONSUMER

Consumer Information Systems (CIS) is a type of information system that provides services to consumers. Instead of appealing to users in traditional organizational environments such as Internet-based television, it is usually formed by using technology, software and as a result of customer interactions. Thanks to this system, it becomes possible to store, distribute and transmit information subject to communication between the company and the customer. Traditional information systems presume that users obtain utilitarian value from firms' offerings. Recently, according to many researchers, customer information systems are defined as a communication system used by members of some human communities, some groups or social actors (Kaufmann H. R. & Panni, 2017, p. 154-155).

According to Reinartz et al. (2004), CRM technology is information technology distributed for better management of customer relations. It includes front office applications that can support sales, marketing and service, as well as a data storage and back office applications that integrate and analyze data about customers. Thus, CRM technology can increase the capabilities of businesses to maintain customer relationships profitably by facilitating customer interactions, analyzing information about profitable customers, designing more efficient and effective processes, and it provide customizing products or services (Whang & Feng, 2012, p. 119).

In this way, businesses get the opportunity to develop long-lasting relationships with customers. In addition, with the help of CRM technology, businesses have obtained a very effective method to prevent possible causes of complaints by receiving timely and objective feedback from their customers. This allows to become aware of existing problems and prevent possible problems by evaluating them from the customer's perspective.

In recent years, mobile marketing has emerged as a new marketing channel for companies to reach customers individually. For marketing managers, this is an effective channel to deliver their message to the customers they want to target. In order to design the most effective CRM strategy, it is also important today that managers understand the basic benefits and make the most of this new communication channel (Kumar & Petersen, 2017, p. 226).

CRM software guides businesses to communicate effectively with their customers, and the main goal of this application is to help businesses understand customer needs and behavior and provide better quality of service

(Paliouras & Siakas, 2017, p. 23).

Conclusion

Because of the nature of the product they offer, service businesses are very often faced with uncertainties, deviations and failures. Because service delivery is unique, it is very difficult to capture a certain standardization, and what is purchased is a process/action, and because they are produced and consumed simultaneously, services also contain some elements of failure. In these elements of failure, which are contrary to the nature of professionalization, the important thing is to be able to effectively compensate for the failure suffered by the customer, as well as the effort to perform an failure-free service delivery at all. Recovery activities maintained in the light of the necessary criteria are likely to face a higher positive return than the current situation if they win the customer's appreciation or approval. A business that approaches mistakes by looking at them from the customer's eyes and displaying a pro-Customer attitude is much more successful in recovery activities and even faces a positive and persistent customer response. As such, the customer's post-recovery Service and business view may be much more positive than that of a customer who did not experience any failures. Therefore, service pricing activities play a very important role in shaping the perspective of customers.

A customer who can qualify as ideal for a business is a customer who needs a problem or need that the business can meet, has the opportunity to buy the business's activities (for example, time and money), and as a result of this purchase, almost becomes a representative of the firm, defending the firm everywhere, depending on it and satisfied with it. As a matter of fact, the main purpose of service failure and service recovery activities is to be able to come to this position with the existing customer.

At this point, being able to communicate with customers and carrying this communication to the dimension of relationship is very important for businesses to better understand customer expectations and to develop business processes that will produce satisfactory results. The customer relationship management system offers an interactive and systematic communication opportunity that offers businesses the chance to get to know their customers better and to make up for any mistakes that may arise in order to make them loyal customers.

Traditional customer relationship management, which has been used and used for a long time, has made a great progress with the development of technology and the acceptance of people over time, and the technology-customer-vendor relationship has been established firmly. Today, the customer profile that we call the post-modern customer has become a mass with reduced tolerance for failure and a tendency to give up very quickly. Therefore, businesses must develop and maintain customer relationships by interacting with customers and managing the information gathered from these interactions. Interactions facilitate communication, and this communication provides the flow of goods or services, including information exchange between a company and its customers. At this point, both employees, all business processes, and all digital media that are indispensable for communication today should be designed in a way to keep the customer relationship experience at the highest level.

It is important that all businesses that define themselves as service businesses plan their work in a way that avoids mistakes as much as possible and provide in-service training to their personnel in this direction. However, it is very important to use the correct communication methods by preparing simulations and plans regarding how to treat customers in case of possible service failure, which techniques should be used to solve the problems and what can be done to satisfy the customer.

Effective management of complaints, which is one of the most important reasons preventing the establishment of a long-term relationship with the customer, will undoubtedly eliminate this obstacle. Therefore, it would not be wrong to say that the complaint management should be effective first for the effectiveness of the CRM and in this way, it will be possible to detect and compensate service failures.

REFERENCES

Bayuk, M. N. (2006). Hizmet pazarlaması ve müşteri tutma, Akademik Bakış Dergisi, 10, 1-12.

Bell, C.R. & Ridge, K. (1992), Service recovery for trainers, Training and Development, 5(46), 58-63.

Bell, C.R. & Zemke, R. E. (1987), Service breakdown: the road to recovery, Management Review, 76(10), 32-35.

Bitner, M. Jo., Booms, B.. H. & Tetreault, M. S. (1990). The service encounter: diagnosing favorable and unfavorable incidents, Journal of Marketing, 54(1), 71-84.

Boshoff, C.(1999), Recovsat: an instrument to measure satisfaction with transaction-specific service recovery, Journal of Service Research, 1(3), 236-249.

Boulding, W., Staelin R., Ehret M. & Johnston W. J. (2005), A customer relationship management roadmap: what is known, potential pitfalls, and where to go, Journal of Marketing, 69 (October), 155-166.

Catalán-Matamoros, D. (2012) Advances in customer relationship management (an overview to customer relationship management), Croatia (Hırvatistan): Intech.

Chang W, Park JE, & Chaiy S (2010) How does crm technology transform into organizational performance? a mediating role of marketing capability, Journal of Business Research, 63(8): 849-55.

Chen, IJ & Popovich K (2003). Understanding customer relationship management (crm)-people, process and technology, Business Process Management Journal, 9(5): 672-88.

Chua, B. L., Othman, M., Boo, H. C., Abkarim, M. S., Ramachandran, S.ridar (2010), Servicescape failure and recovery strategy in the fast food service industry: the effect of costumer repatronization, Journal of Quality Assurance in Hospitality and Tourism, 11(3), 179-198.

Coltman, T., (2007). Can superior crm capabilities improve performance in banking, Journal of Financial Services Marketing, 12(2): 102-14.

Chuang, S.-H., & Lin, H.-N. (2013). The roles of infrastructure capability and customer orientation in enhancing customer-information quality in crm systems: Empirical evidence from Taiwan. International Journal of Information Management, 33(2), 271–281.

Clark. M. & Melancon, J. (2013). The influence of social media investment on relational outcomes: a relationship marketing perspective, International Journal of Marketing Studies; 5 (4): 132-142.

Ennew, C. & Schoefer, K. (2003), Service failure and service recovery in tourism: a review, E. Koc (eds.), in service failures and recovery in tourism and hospitality (2-16), Oxford: CABI.

Eren, D. (2015), Konaklama pazarlamasında hizmet aksamalarını önleme ve düzeltme, B. Kılıç ve Z.Öter (eds.), Turizm pazarlamasında güncel yaklaşımlar içinde (589-618), İstanbul: Beta Yayıncılık.

Garrido-Moreno, A., & Padilla-Meléndez, A. (2011). Analyzing the impact of knowledge management on crm success: the mediating effects of organizational factors, International Journal of Information Management, 31(5), 437–444.

Grönroos, C. (1988), Service quality: the six criteria of good perceived service quality, Review of Business, 9 (3), 10-13.

Grönroos, C. (1990), Relationship marketing approach to the marketing function in service context: the marketing and organizational behaviour influence. Journal of Business Research, 20 (1), 3-20.

Grönroos. C. (1991), The marketing strategy continuum: toward a marketing conceit for the service marketing, Service Marketing Management Decision, (29), 1-12.

Gülmez M. & Kitapçı, O. (2003). İlişki pazarlamasının gelişimi ve yakın geleceği, Cumhuriyet Üniversitesi İ.İ.B.F. Dergisi, 4 (2), 82.

Gümüş, S. (2012). Hizmet, hizmet pazarlaması, Türkiye'de bireysel emeklilik sistemi ve pazarlama stratejileri. İstanbul: Hiperlink.

Günaydın Ö.I. & Işık D. A. (2017). Uluslarası ticaret işletmelerinde karşılaşılan hizmet hatalarının belirlenmesi: nitel bir araştırma. Uluslararası Yönetim İktisat ve İsletme Dergisi, ICMEB17 Özel Sayısı: 243.

Habul A., Pilav-Velić, A. & Kremić, E (2012). Customer relationship management and business intelligence, Advances in Customer Relationship Management. Rijeka: InTech Europe, 13-30.

Hirshman, A.O. (1970), Exit, voice and loyalty responses to decline in firms, organizations and states, Cambridge: Harvard University Press.

Hoffman, K. Douglas, K., Scott W. & Rotalsky, H.M. (1995), Tracking service failures and employee recovery efforts, Journal of Services Marketing, 9(2), 49-61.

Kaufmann H. R. & Panni M. F. A. K. (2017) Socio-economic perspectives on consumer engagement and buying behavior, USA: IGI Global.

Keaveney, S.M. (1995). Costumer switching behaviour in service industries: an exploratory study, Journal of Marketing, 59(2), 71-82.

Keith, R.A. & Jones, E. (2008). Customer relationship management: finding value drivers. Industrial Marketing Management. 37, 120–130.

Kırım, A. (2001), Strateji ve bire-bir pazarlama, İstanbul: Sistem Yayıncılık.

Kumar V. & Petersen J.A (2012). Statistical methods in customer relationship management, USA: John Wiley & Sons.

Kwon, S.Y. & Jang, S.C. (2012), Effects of compensation for service recovery: from theory perspective, International Journal of Hospitality Management, (31), 1235-1243.

Zemke, R. & Bell, C. (1990). Service recovery: Doing it right the second time. Training. 27, 42-48.

Landon, L. E. Jr. (1977), A model of consumers' complaint behaviour, R.L. (ed.) in Day, consumer satisfaction, dissatisfaction and complaining behavior. Papers from a Marketing research Symposium, School of business, Indiana University, Bloomington, April (20-22), 31-35.

Lewis B. R. & McCann P. (2004). Service failure and recovery: evidence from the hotel industry. International Journal of Comtemporary Hospitality Management. 16: 7.

Lovelock, C. & Wirtz J. (2011), Services marketing: people, technology, strategy, Pearson Prentice Hall.

Matos, C. A., Henrique, J. L. & Rossi, C. A. V. (2007), Service recovery paradox: a meta-analysis, Journal of Service Research, 10(1), 60-77.

McCollough, M. A. & Bharadwaj, S. G. (1992). The recovery paradox: an examination of consumer satisfaction in relation to disconfirmation, service quality, and attribution based theories, Marketing Theory and Applications, 3, 119.

McDougall, G. H. G. & Levesque, T. J. (1999). Waiting for Service: Effectiveness of Recovery Strategies, International Journal of Contemporary Hospitality Management, 11(1), 6-15.

Miller J. L., Craighead C.W. & Karwan K. R. (2000). Service recovery: a framework and empirical investigation. Journal of Operations Management. 18: 387-400.

Mueller, H., & Nyfeler, T. (2011). Quality in patent information retrieval – communication as the key factor. World Paten Information, 33(4), 383–388.

Mueller, R. D., Palmer, A., Mack, R., McMullan, R. (2003), Service in the restaurant industry: an American and Irish comprasion of service failures and recovery strategies, Hospitality Management, 22, 395-418.

Nguyen, D.T. & McColl-Kennedy, J.R. (2003), Diffusing costumer anger in service recovery: a conceptual framework, Australasian Marketing Journal, 11(2), 46-55.

Ok, C, Back, Ki-J. & Shanklin, C. W. (2007), Mixed findings on the service recovery paradox, The Service Industries Journal, 27(6), 671-686.

Öztürk S. A. (2009). Hizmet pazarlaması. Bursa: Ekin Basım.

Paliouras, K., & Siakas, K. V. (2017), Social customer relationship management: a case study. International Journal of Entrepreneurial Knowledge, 5(1), 20–34.

Palmatier, R. W., Rajiv P. Dant, D. G. & Kenneth R. E. (2006). Factors Influencing the effectiveness of relationship marketing: a meta-analysis, Journal of Marketing, 70 (4), 136-153.

Parasuraman, A. P, Berry, L. L. & Zeithaml, V. A., (1991), Understanding customer expectations of service, MIT Sloan Management Review, 32,

39-48.

Payne, A. & Frow P. (2005), Customer relationship management: from strategy to implementation, Journal of Marketing Management, 22, 135-168.

Reinartz, J., Thomas, S. & Kumar, V., (2004). Balancing acquisition and retention resources to maximize customer profitability. Journal of Marketing, 69, 63-79.

Schoefer, K. (2008), The role of cognition and affect in the formation of customer satisfaction judgements concerning service recovery encounters, Journal of Consumer Behaviour, 7, 210-221.

Shostack, G. L. (1984), Designing services that deliver, Boston, McGraw-Hill: Harvard Business Review.

Swanson, S. R. & Hsu, M. K. (2009), Critical incidents in tourism: failure, recovery, customer switching, and word-of-mouth behaviors, Journal of Travel and Tourism Marketing, 26 (2), 180-194.

Schweikhart, S. B., Strasser, S. & Kennedy, M. R. (1993), Service recovery in health services firms, Hospital and Health Services Administration, 38, 3-21.

Vázquez-Casielles, R., Iglesias V. & Varela-Neira C. (2012), Service recovery, satisfaction and behaviour intentions: analysis of compensation and social comparison communication strategies, The Service Industries Journal, 32(1), 83-103.

Xu Y, Yen DC, Lin B & Chou DC. (2002), Adopting customer relationship management technology, Industrial Management & Data Systems, 102 (8): 442-452.

Wang, Y., & Feng, H. (2012). Customer relationship management capabilities, Management Decision, (1), 115–129.

Zeithaml, V.A. & Bitner, M. J. (2003), Services Marketing, McGraw-Hill.

CHAPTER 3

THE ROLE OF SOCIAL MEDIA ON TOURISM MARKETING

Didem DEMİR
Lect., Dr.
Toros University, Department of International Trade and Logistics
didem.demir@toros.edu.tr
orcid.org/0000-0003-4589-8240

Abstract

There are a lot of social media tools that people collaborate each other for many subjects. One of the main subjects that they search, organize, share and ask eachother is about tourism. Social media has a great impact on online marketing and tourists' decisions. Social media commitment and interactivity both effect consumer behavior and management side operationally and strategically for tourism related activities. Main sites like Facebook, Instagram, YouTube, TripAdvisor and Flickr alllow both consumers and tourism marketers come together under a single roof. The effect of social media is higher than mass media advertising during the whole travel planning process. Social media tools play a role to increase the awareness of customers and to change their bahavior towards their choices. Negative and positive customer reviews frequently effect the consumers during their decison process. As a result, while social media effects the consumers decisions, tourism marketers can also benefit from social media engagement at the same time.

Key Words: *Social Media, Tourism Marketing, Values, Consumer Engagement, Decision Making Process*

Introduction

Consumers engage with tourism brands and tourism activities to a greater extent by using social media channels. Gathering information, selecting, booking becomes more accessible by using social media. There is a growing number of social media electronic tools that allow people to collaborate on various subjects. One of the main subjects that they search, organize, share and ask each other about is tourism. Main sites like Facebook, Instagram, YouTube, Trip Advisor and Flickr gather consumers and tourism marketers

https://doi.org/10.2478/9788366675247-003

under a single roof. Technological tools like social media can be used by more consumers if they are aware of its usefulness. As tourism-related products are consumed simultaneously and as they are intangible, social media constitutes a significant platform where tourism consumers can review online information about tourism and hospitality products. Once decision-making process is enhanced by online technology, it prevents making wrong decisions in accordance with the consumers' lifestyle. Moreover, whilst social media affects the decisions of the consumers, tourism marketers also benefit from the consumers' social media engagement. Therefore, it is crucial to analyze the significance of social media for tourism marketing, both from consumers and suppliers' point of view in order to benefit from it in an ever-changing digital environment.

1. Social Media and Tourism Marketing

According to Hudson, Roth, Madden (2012) social media is one of the digital marketing communication options where consumers can interact with each other by sharing information and their experiences. There are also other options like websites, mobile marketing, internet-specific ads, videos, display ads, online communities, interstitials, blogs, and e-mails. While setting the digital marketing strategies, the communication style to promote the products or services is more important than the subject of promotion.

Consumers use the travel planning process and suppliers concentrate on promotion, management, and research functions on social media (Leung, Law, Hoof, & Buhalis, 2013, p. 3). Social media has a strategic importance for tourism competitiveness because it helps simply visibility of tourism organizations on social media. Salkhordeh (2009) searched for the effect of usage of social media for tourism marketing in many ways. He argued about the effects of social media and he thought that it is a crucial tool for strengthening customer loyalty to brands, creating strong and effective customer relations and having the power of attracting potential customers and receiving prompt feedback from existing customers.

Social media enables individuals to share their common interests and activities with new information systems and let them communicate with both friends and other people. People share their interests and the activities that they are involved in by simply chatting and sharing photos and videos. Tourism managers also can facilitate by spreading information online especially about their promotional activities for tourism marketing (Miguéns,

Baggio and Costa,2008, p.1).

Decision-making process of consumers highly depends on the products or services that they intend to buy. For instance, making a decision for buying a touristic tour package differs from going to a grocery for buying something. Purchasing a holiday involves a high amount of income and time. There are many internal and external motivators and determinants as tourism consumers try to make their choices. These internal motivators and determinants depend on personality, health, income, family, work commitments, hobbies, interests, lifestyle, attitudes, opinions, perceptions, past experiences and also existing knowledge of potential holidays. On the other hand, tourists' external motivations are based on e-word of mouth, special promotions, information obtained from tourism destinations and media, advice of travel agents, availability of suitable tourism products and services, the climate of tourism regions, health problems, visa requirements and sometimes political restrictions. In such situations the managers should understand why and how the consumers make their final decisions and it is also very important to understand consumers' needs and wants according to their demand for tourism products and services. This will also lead organizations to develop these kinds of products and services which are appropriately positioned for their target market (Horner and Swarbrooke, 2016, p.4-5). Tourist behavior also depends on the type of tourism that they are involved in. The main types of tourism are as followed:

1. Visiting friends and relatives
2. Scenic tourism
3. Business tourism
4. Cultural tourism
5. Educational tourism
6. Social tourism
7. Religious tourism
8. Health tourism

Tourists care reliability and simplicity that they perceive and they participate according to interactivity when they perceive it much wider and varied (Olga Lo, P., & Razaq, R. 2014). There are four stages of touristic encouragement and these stages are recorded as attention, interest, desire, and action. According to this model (AIDA), attention is the first step that tourism providers try to attract customers for their tourism products and services while they are on the purchase decision process (Alghizzawi, Salloum and Habes,

2018). If a person is socialized interactively his/her interest will occur during the decision process. A successful market manager needs to solve all problems of the tourism company for increasing the benefit. Desire is an attitude related to people's needs and wants. Creating desire in the consumer's mind would be the success of the marketing manager when they intend to buy that tourism service. Finally, an individual's decision is based on acting in the last step, they take action according to what they perceive from social media platforms of touristic companies.

When it comes to tourism brands it is so important to build up a tourism brand that reveals customer engagement on social media. Customer loyalty is the result of customer engagement and brand managers should dwell on two things to handle this situation. One of them is taking part in social media and the other one is evolving strategies for assuring customer engagement on social media channels. The way of doing these strategies may be providing recreational, hilarious, or scholastic themes through social media to absorb customers. These interactions can help brand managers to create a unique image for the identification of their brand on others. In addition to this being honest and clear can be a good way of building positive customer engagement on social media while replying to customers' questions. Tourism customers absorb, identify and interact with a specific brand with some functions such as sharing pictures, videos, questionnaires and comments related to the aforementioned brand (Harrigan, Evers, Miles, and Daly, 2017).

Verma and McCarthy (2012) carried out a research about the hospitality industry in relation to social media in which 2830 travelers participated. According to the findings of the study, women read more reviews of consumers' experiences on Trip Advisor compared to men. Moreover, while men like to read professional reviews, women prefer to read both professional reviews and customer reviews on social media like Instagram and Tripadvisor.

Fotis, Buhalis, and Rossides (2011) performed a study with 346 online internet users who use social media to plan their vacation. They found out that consumers mostly use social media to share their experiences after holidays and they also intend to change their holiday plans just because their ideas are influenced by social media. It is also noted that user-generated content that is shared on social media is more trusted by other consumers in comparison to the traditional contents of travel agencies and mass media advertising channels.

Öz (2015) stated that the value of tourism companies' brand name increases by sharing photos and videos consistently on social media. Boosting the reliability of the company, these social media interactions give rise to a positive e-wom (electronic word of mouth) and enable companies to reach out to more prospective consumers.

Digital users have the advantage of using social media to get information about touristic destinations' reputations and they can also integrate all kinds of information and data during their journey. They can even analyze the reports according to the ranking of hotels in the hospitality industry. Many consumers prefer social media just because it is low-cost and bias-free (Živković, Gajić, and Brdar ,2014, p. 760).

According to Expectation Theory customers compare the performance of a product or a service with the standards of the performance determined before. If the consumer's perception of the performance exceeds his/her previous expectation, the customer is satisfied. If the performance is neutral, then the result is zero disconfirmation. Finally, negative disconfirmation leads to unsatisfied consumers (Kahneman and Tversky, 2013). In their study, Narangajavana, Fiol, Tena, Artola, and García (2017) surveyed the influence of social media in creating expectations to select tourist destinations. They deduced that the consumers trust the user-generated content shared by the others and although they have no idea about the person who shared that content, those sources and supporting ideas meet their expectations. Finally, consumers who use social media for planning their journeys feel happy with the destination that they choose as the disconfirmation theory clarifies (Nguyen, de Leeuw, and Dullaert, 2018).

In his research about social media's effects on tourism, Bay (2018) comes up with the positive relations of significant results of social media that it has a significant impact on both tourism and consumer behavior.

2. Creating Value On Social Media for Tourism Marketing

Zeitahaml (1988) defines perceived value for consumers as what is received and what is given for the utility of the consumers. Holbrook (1999) expresses different kinds of perceived value and these values are summarized as follows:

1. Efficiency is a perceived value depends on the usage of something for a specific purpose. Consumers' perceived value is dependent on getting the maximum amount of convenience and minimum amount of spending time, money, and energy.

2. Excellence is customers' perceived value both based on satisfaction and quality according to their expectations.

3. Status is the other value based on how other people perceive one's image.

4. Esteem is how one's possessions reflect the others.

5. Play value is like only one's pure pleasure and it is an experience that is motivated intrinsically.

6. Aesthetics is valued intrinsically only for its pleasant look instead of its utility.

7. Ethics is valued as its benefit to other people such as using environmental products or services.

8. Spirituality is a value involving mystic or inner power for one's own sake.

These values play an important role in the decision making process for tourism consumers. Customers kind of interaction on web-sites influence their value perception. What they utilize and the experience form the web pages influence their value perception and it important to consider the customers' relations with each other for creating the expected value (Lexhagen ,2009, p.51).

Building customer value depends on strategic decisions that companies need to achieve especially in the digital environment. The digital quotient of the company shows effectiveness in implementing long-term digital life and the power of the corporate infrastructure and technological knowledge. Additionally, it helps to monitor the digital capabilities, targeted investments and digital growth of a company. Using big data enables creating various content for companies like catalogs, coupons, web pages, mobile applications just to increase customer experiences. This allows companies to analyze their segmentation strategies, workflow, and also help them run their internal and external operations much more properly.

Social interaction value is perceived in accordance with the expansion and care of relations with the community. There are some social cues that provide social interaction value, such as interactivity and communication between consumers and tourism suppliers. These clues can be summarized as the visual appearance of the company on the internet such as the photos, videos, layout, colors or music appearing on their own online profile. These are the things that attract and satisfy customers. Aesthetic cues used on online platforms like social media also encourage the return on investment of the company. Identity attractiveness is another social cue for the consumers; social media helps to create this effect between users and brands and some people internalize the brand as they identify the features of that brand corresponding with themselves (Pérez-Vega, Taheri, Farrington and O'Gorman2018).

Yen and Teng (2015) examined the role of perceived value with 382 tourism consumers in Taiwan and they examined the mediation role of perceived value both for behavioral intentions and celebrity involvement. They found out that destination marketers should consider celebrities as a positive pull factor for travel destinations to create value for travelers. It is just like an evidence to deal with celebrities in social media channels while delivering tourism products and services. On the other hand, destination marketers should be aware of the ethical and moral image of celebrities to prevent negative effects while promoting the travel destination.

Chung and Koo (2015) accomplished research with 695 travelers about the use of social media for searching travel information. They concluded that traveler's value of social media is ruling the usage of social media. Social media users especially search for getting information and they are affected by both reliability of information and enjoyment as benefits. In their research, they only find enjoyment as a dimension that makes a direct impact on social media usage. However, they sacrifice complexity and perceived effort while using social media for searching tourism activities. Thus, the managers should use a much more user-friendly interface while creating their pages or while starting an application about their tourism activities.

3. The Effect of Social Media for Tourism Marketing

By the development of technology the rise in the use of computers and smart phones and increased time spend on the internet ensures social marketing activities as well as marketing efforts on online platforms (Arıkan and Marangoz, 2018, p. 143).

Social media is preferred to classic media as people can reach all the information about destination research and disseminate it to others easier and faster. User-generated content is also called social networking. Likes and clicks of consumers on online comments, photographs, videos about tourism products and services let other potential consumers get a glimpse of these remixture ideas and experiences for every step of their journey. By using GPS location, both friends and family can be aware of where you are, what you are doing by using the features of smart phones or tablets on social media networks. Moreover, when you go somewhere you can get a recommendation of that destination's touristic places like restaurants, hotels, or museums based on your GPS location (Manap and Adzharudin, 2013). Social media allows all consumers to receive and to generate their feelings, opinions, suggestions, and compliments both verbally, visually, and auditorily.

According to Law, Buhalis, Cobanoglu (2014) it is important to use new technologies like virtual reality and 3D while designing the web sites of different tourism destinations. It can be helpful for managers to formulate new business models and marketing strategies. Moreover, it can also be useful to provide new technologies like applications that can help consumers while they are travelling. Consumers tend to search their needs and desires effectively through social media where people share their activities by text messages, pictures, or videos in real-time and by word-of-mouth. For managers, it is not easy to control travel products in advance and social media lets them to make their promotional activities in a much more cost-effective way (Chung & Koo, 2015). Usage of the internet enables to transform technology for the implementation of marketing of goods and services on virtual platforms. Therefore, it also helps to build unexplored working patterns for the managers where the internet increases the customer value and also lets them to increase profitability for both the private and public sectors. Consequently, like the other sectors tourism organizations using blogs are able to reach different global markets for making international agreements (Akehurst, 2009, s. 52).

Marketing managers can place ads about travel applications on social media through which consumers can be directed to those applications. These persuasive advertising techniques increase competitively whileoffering tourism products and services (Živković, Gajić and Brdar ,2014, p. 760). On social media platforms, online networks are heterogeneous so web-assisted decision-making behavior should be designed according to target group segmentation. It is also important to find out accurate information that is needed to help the consumers make positive decisions. Apart from this, tourism providers should create a uniformed content providing cooperation and involvement among consumers on their social media platforms instead of sending constant messages. The managers can also stimulate consumers by sharing real-time scenarios created by existing customers. A technological set-up like wi-fi access, digital hotel activities and video shares are also substantial for getting positive evaluations from the consumers (Gupta, 2019).

Zeng and Gerritsen (2014) stated that social media has a high impact on especially information search and decision making process for potential tourists. It is also effective for promotional activities of many destinations for the managers and marketers. Edelman (2010) discussed the way of using marketing budget on social media and they claimed that it is more profitable to use the marketing budget on the stages of enjoyment, advocating and bonding for tourism sector instead of the stages of consideration and procurement.

Consumers often share their ideas and experiences after the purchasing process. (Hudson and Thal, 2013, p. 156). The consumer decision process to purchase something can be listed in four stages (Lecinski, 2011):

1. Considering
2. Evaluating
3. Buying
4. Advocating and bonding

During the decision process, "evaluating" and "advocating" stages are increasingly relevant to social media. Unplanned purchasing behavior has become a very important source of income for businesses (Biçer, Yıldız, & Sarıtepe, p. 203). Innovations and developments in the communication world have also caused some changes in the shopping behavior of consumers. In parallel, businesses have started to respond not only to the physiological demands of the consumers but also to their emotional wishes. This is because today's postmodern companies have turned to customers who have an expectation of abstract benefits rather than tangible benefits and who can make instant decisions as a result of the payment facilities provided by the businesses. In addition, Aichner (2012) claims that marketing can be an interactive tool by using tools like laptops, tablets or smartphones because they let the consumers interact with the products through communication technologies via the internet. This creates value for customers when they are trying to decide for something although they do not see or touch the product yet, but tend to buy them via the internet by searching especially on social media. Podcasting is also a social media tool that is issued by a personal perspective. Podcasts that relate to tourism activities are often tagged by 'travel' and 'tourism' that consumers can focus on travel plans, journey experiences, accommodation variety and advice or activities in those touristic destinations. Podcasts are generalized in three groups as destination podcasts, travel experience podcasts, travel and tourism industry podcasts. These are all about the insights, experiences, and advice of people from their perspective (Feifan Xie, Lew, 2008, p. 174). These podcasts affect the consumer's attraction to tourism destinations, especially during their decision process.

In their qualitative study, Chatzigeorgiou and Christou (2020) stated that consumers experience both negative and positive experiences while using social media distribution services for the tourism sector. The consumers usually access through social media for making reservations and also for purchasing different kinds of tourism products and services like booking, organizing and purchasing transformation and hotel accommodation services, etc. The consumers sometimes have difficulty for applying the directions given while purchasing something online and some of the consumers complain about their smart phones since they don't carry out online transactions with their existing smart phones just because they don't include enough technology proceed online. Besides this, some of the consumers are satisfied with the online transaction because they feel free to search and buy tourism products and services without time pressure, they can do their transactions 24 hours a day. They are also satisfied with the speed and opportunity to access any offers to make up their holiday package.

Travelers access various social media tools for discovering online information for each stage of their journey (Verma et al., 2012). It is so important for hotels to create their content for integrating their digital infrastructure on social media. Moreover, user-led content allows prospective consumers to be aware of real-time posts shared by the existing consumers via Facebook, Instagram or Twitter. These can guide and influence the customers positively and cause them to select the aforementioned hotel. Engagement and reward strategies like an opportunity to comment about the hotel or leave reviews can also affect the potential consumers positively (Varkaris and Neuhofer, 2017). Beyond the positive role of social media it could be a problem that it is possible for both hotel managers and tourism consumers to be affected negatively if the content of social media is not proper.

Social media enables popular trends and these digital movements inspire electronic word of mouth. This has an effect of increasing customer loyalty in connecting with high corporate sales and profit. These steps occurring on social media are crucial both for travelers while planning the steps of their journeys and for tourism providers to understand what's happening outside of their hotel, travel agency or airline, etc. They have the opportunity to define the opportunities and threats coming from the outside as they exist online on social media (Minazzi, 2015). Consumers search for getting information, making decisions, sharing their positive or negative experiences on social media. Consumers perception changes according to what is shared thus tourism providers should take an action for their future managerial functions and practices as social media exists (Sotiriadis, 2017). This indicates that every marketer can set up their strategies based on digital platforms on social media and be aware of the others before taking an action. For instance, managers should follow their competitors on social media and try to overcome the feedback given by the tourism consumers related to the company but they should also be aware of the feedback given about the other companies so as to take those responses as a pattern to apply.

Discovering "stores or other places to shop" , "potential destinations to visit", "information about a specific location", "places to stay or hotel prices", "air ticket and timetable/flight time" are known as the most clicks rated on the internet while trying to make travel plans. (Huang, Goo, Nam & Yoo 2017). Hence social connections information which are attached as "on top of users" and "online reviews made by the others" will be appealing for the potential tourism consumers who are seeking for information for their vacation (Kim, Lee, Shin, & Yang 2017).

Discussions and feedback process on social media is critical during the decision process of potential customers who are searching for tourism activities (Olga Lo, P., & Razaq, R. 2014). E-wom strategies for social media depend on two things. One of them is informational and the other one is revenue-generating. If the exchange of information is positive, it creates credibility for the organizations. Nevertheless, the opposite can create a negative case when the customers are dissatisfied. If the customers have problems and doubts on their mind, complaints will be destructive for the company's informational strategy because of perceived negativity. On the other hand, positive e-wom strategies also decrease the expenses for the marketing department and increase the revenue if customers are active on social media. A better image of the company on social media also generates revenue (Filieri and McLeay, 2014).

While sharing the information firms should pay attention to the things as follows:

1. Prosperity and depth of the information obtained
2. Straightforward and simplicity of usage of the information
3. Accessibility at any time

The findings suggest that there is evidence of consumers concern while getting information online listed as:

1. Reliability and acceptability of the information given online
2. Privacy of the consumers
3. An excessive load or amount of information
4. Insufficient resources on the internet
5. Lack of knowledge and lack of skills in technology use (Milano, Baggio and Piattelli, 2011)

Conclusion

Consumers gathered information about tourism from travel agents, newspapers, brochures or magazines before the age of social media. However, these were the limited resources for searching price, place and the service given for all tourism activities like accommodation, food and beverage, transformation, leisure activities, etc. As internet became inseparable from our lives, social media gained importance and social media channels like Instagram, Facebook and Tripadvisor modified the way consumers acquire information.

In the tourism and hospitality field people use social media to share their travel-related ideas, problems and experiences, they contact each other, connect with other people to share photos and videos and they also intend to buy products and services related to tourism and hospitality via social media channels through electronic word-of-mouth (e-wom). As mentioned before value is defined as perceived benefits minus perceived costs for the customers and when these values are classified as hedonic and utilitarian value, they both can enable positive purchase intentions for tourism products and services associated by social media engagement.

Research studies in academic literature underline the importance of using social media properly both for managers and consumers. Arguing the importance of social media for tourism marketing and creating value for customers on social media, the present study is expected to contribute to the existing literature in the theoretical sense.

REFERENCES

Aichner, T. (2012). The zero moment of truth in mass customization. International Journal of Industrial Engineering and Management, 3(4), 173-178.

Akehurst, G. (2009). User generated content: the use of blogs for tourism organisations and tourism consumers. Service business, 3(1), 51.

Alghizzawi, M., Salloum, S. A., & Habes, M. (2018). The role of social media in tourism marketing in Jordan. International Journal of Information Technology and Language Studies, 2(3), 59-70.

Arıkan, Ö. U., & Marangoz, A. Y. (2018). Sosyal Pazarlama Kavramı Ve Sosyal Pazarlamada Sosyal Medya Kullanımı: Sağlık Kampanyaları Uygulamaları. Toros Üniversitesi İİSBF Sosyal Bilimler Dergisi, 5(8), 141-165.

Bay, S. W. (2018). The effects of social media on consumer behaviour in tourism: A study among university students (Doctoral dissertation, UTAR).

Biçer, D. F., Yıldız, S. Y., & Sarıtepe, Ö. K. Mobil Alışveriş Uygulamaları Kullanan Bireylerin Satın Alma Davranışları. Yönetim ve Ekonomi Araştırmaları Dergisi, 17(3), 201-221.

Chatzigeorgiou, C., & Christou, E. (2020). Adoption of social media as distribution channels in tourism marketing: A qualitative analysis of consumers' experiences. Journal of Tourism, Heritage & Services Marketing, 6(1), 25-32.

Chung, N., & Koo, C. (2015). The use of social media in travel information search. Telematics and Informatics, 32(2), 215-229.

Kahneman, D., & Tversky, A. (2013). Prospect theory: An analysis of decision under risk. In Handbook of the fundamentals of financial decision making: Part I (pp. 99-127).

Edelman, D. C. (2010). Branding in the digital age. Harvard business review, 88(12), 62-69.

Feifan Xie, P., & Lew, A. A. (2008). Podcasting and tourism: An exploratory study of types, approaches, and content. Information Technology & Tourism, 10(2), 173- 180.

Filieri, R., & McLeay, F. (2014). E-WOM and accommodation: An analysis of the factors that influence travelers' adoption of information from online reviews. Journal of Travel Research, 53(1), 44-57

Fotis, J., Buhalis, D., & Rossides, N. (2011). Social media impact on holiday travel planning: The case of the Russian and the FSUmarkets. International Journal of Online Marketing (IJOM), 1(4), 1-19.

Gretzel, U., Koo, C., Sigala, M., & Xiang, Z. (2015). Special issue on smart tourism: convergence of information technologies, experiences, and theories. Electronic Markets, 25(3), 175-177.

Gretzel, U., & Yoo, K. H. (2013). Premises and promises of social media marketing in tourism. The Routledge handbook of tourism marketing, 491-504.

Gupta, V. (2019). The influencing role of social media in the consumer's hotel decision-making process. Worldwide Hospitality and Tourism Themes.

Harrigan, P., Evers, U., Miles, M., & Daly, T. (2017). Customer engagement with tourism social media brands. Tourism management, 59, 597-609.

Horner, S., & Swarbrooke, J. (2016). Consumer behaviour in tourism. Routledge.

Huang, C. D., Goo, J., Nam, K., & Yoo, C. W. (2017). Smart tourism technologies in travel planning: The role of exploration and exploitation. Information & Management, 54(6), 757-770.

Hudson, S., Roth, M. S., & Madden, T. J. (2012). Customer

communications management in the new digital era. Center for marketing studies, Darla moore school of business, University of south Carolina, 21.

Hudson, S., & Thal, K. (2013). The impact of social media on the consumer decision process: Implications for tourism marketing. Journal of Travel & Tourism Marketing, 30(1-2), 156-160.

Kim, S. E., Lee, K. Y., Shin, S. I., & Yang, S. B. (2017). Effects of tourism information quality in social media on destination image formation: The case of Sina Weibo. Information & management, 54(6), 687-702.

Law, R., Buhalis, D., & Cobanoglu, C. (2014). Progress on information and communication technologies in hospitality and tourism. International Journal of Contemporary Hospitality Management.

Lecinksi, J. (2011). Winning the zero moment of truth. Zero Moment of Truth.

Leung, D., Law, R., Van Hoof, H., & Buhalis, D. (2013). Social media in tourism and hospitality: A literature review. Journal of travel & tourism marketing, 30(1-2), 3-22.

Lexhagen, M. (2009). Customer perceived value of travel and tourism web sites. International Journal of Information Systems in the Service Sector (IJISSS), 1(1), 35-53.

Manap, K. A., & Adzharudin, N. A. (2013, January). The role of user generated content (UGC) in social media for tourism sector. In The 2013 WEI international academic conference proceedings (pp. 52-58).

Miguéns, J., Baggio, R., & Costa, C. (2008). Social media and tourism destinations: TripAdvisor case study. Advances in tourism research, 26(28), 1-6.

Milano, R., Baggio, R., & Piattelli, R. (2011, January). The effects of online social media on tourism websites. In ENTER (pp. 471-483).
Minazzi, R. (2015). Social media marketing in tourism and hospitality.

Narangajavana, Y., Fiol, L. J. C., Tena, M. Á. M., Artola, R. M. R., & García, J. S. (2017). The influence of social media in creating expectations. An empirical study for a tourist destination. Annals of Tourism Research, 65, 60-70.

Nguyen, D. H., de Leeuw, S., & Dullaert, W. E. (2018). Consumer behavior and order fulfillment in online retailing: a systematic review. International Journal of Management Reviews, 20(2), 255-276.

Olga Lo, P., & Razaq, R. (2014). Evolution of social media and consumer behavior changes in tourism destination promotion. International Journal of Business and Globalisation, 12(3), 358-368.

Öz, M. (2015). Social media utilization of tourists for travel-related purposes. International Journal of Contemporary Hospitality Management.

Pérez-Vega, R., Taheri, B., Farrington, T., & O'Gorman, K. (2018). On being attractive, social, and visually appealing in social media: The effects of anthropomorphic tourism brands on Facebook fan pages. Tourism management, 66, 339-347.

Salkhordeh, P. (2011). Key issues in the use of social networking in the hospitality industry: 2009.

Sotiriadis, M. D. (2017). Sharing tourism experiences in social media. International Journal of Contemporary Hospitality Management.

Varkaris, E., & Neuhofer, B. (2017). The influence of social media on the consumers' hotel decision journey. Journal of Hospitality and Tourism Technology.

Verma, R., Stock, D., & McCarthy, L. (2012). Customer preferences for online, social media, and mobile innovations in the hospitality industry. Cornell Hospitality Quarterly, 53(3), 183-186.

Yen, C. H., & Teng, H. Y. (2015). Celebrity involvement, perceived value, and behavioral intentions in popular media-induced tourism. Journal of Hospitality & Tourism Research, 39(2), 225-244.

Zeng, B., & Gerritsen, R. (2014). What do we know about social media in tourism? A review. Tourism management perspectives, 10, 27-36.

CHAPTER 4

ADVERTISING POSTERS AND COMMUNICATION THROUGH METAPHORS

İbrahim Gökhan CEYLAN
Assoc. Prof. Dr.
Sinop University, Gerze Vocational School, Department of Design
gokhanceylan@sinop.edu.tr
orcid.org/0000-0002-6692-8827

Abstract

The advertising posters are one of the mass communication means that are pretty effective in terms of conveying the characteristics of the products that they advertise to the consumers in a very short amount of time and persuading the consumers. Such effective advertising tools transform into an effective advertising strategy for the designers by increasing their power more along with a metaphoric approach. The indirect and powerful narrative of the metaphor grabs the attention of the consumer when compared to the ordinary advertising posters and allows the consumers to think about the message which is intended to be given. In this study, the compatibility of the metaphor with the target audience will be evaluated by examining the examples of the use of metaphors in the advertising posters and the messages that they want to convey to the audiences.

Key Words: *Visual Communication, Graphic Design, Semiology, Metaphors, Advertisiment.*

Introduction

With the purpose of this study being to discuss the metaphorical approaches that are used most often in advertising poster designs, it will be appropriate to first address the question of what advertising is. Both the emergence of advertising with the beginning of trade and the need for advertising date back to older times than one would think. Graphic design is just one of the many areas that have arisen and subsequently grown in parallel with the need for advertising.

https://doi.org/10.2478/9788366675247-004

"Interpersonal communication has existed ever since humanity came into existence. Likewise, advertising dates back to ancient times when trade began. Even though the components of advertising have been made use of ever since antiquity, environments of advertising started to alter over time with the changing needs of people and progress in technology. As a result, advertising designs rapidly turned into visual designs which led to an increase in both the influence spheres and memorability of ads."
(Ceylan and Ceylan, 2019, p. 95).

As is the case for communication, visual designs also underwent changes from one period to another in terms of the ways in which thoughts are conveyed to audience. In the course of time, the need to convey messages to audience and the way and necessity to arouse a target feeling in audience developed into an objective that needed be devised even prior to aesthetic concerns. Hence, designers started to tend towards producing visual works based on metaphorical thinking to convey more meaning with less visuals, making use of metaphorical approaches with a multitude of interwoven meanings contained within, rather than direct illustration.

According to Eraslan (2011), whose research we studied to explain the concept of metaphor, metaphors are the conceptual effects that people develop towards concepts or events and phenomena. When considered in semantic terms, it is the effects and expressions created in people by these concepts, events and phenomena (Eraslan, 2011, p. 17).

When designing posters for advertising campaigns, effective elements are needed that will enable the product or service reach the target audience. With the increase in communication channels available to audience, the creativity and effectiveness of posters have gained ever-increasing importance with each passing day. Posters created to contain metaphorical elements are providing considerable competitive advantage while ensuring positive communication with audience. Verbal metaphors created by various wordplays and visual metaphors consisting of surprising visuals that make the audience think are becoming a primary source to strengthen the designer's hand. Therefore, it is necessary to examine and evaluate what position today's posters that are fed from these sources and provide a kind of message exchange between the designer and audience hold in the current system, and to understand the meanings and ideas today's designers associate with their work. This is where semiotics steps in, because implicit meanings intended to be given by association are assigned to the created poster designs by way of metaphorical approaches.

Semiotics, when dealing with a meaningful whole together with all its meaning generation processes, examines the ways in which the semantic layers of an addressed product that comprise a whole are added to that whole. The areas of analysis can be a writing, an image, a theater play or a musical piece. It is possible to say that meanings conveyed by images are more efficient than those conveyed by words (Ardıç Çobaner, 2013, p. 220). And obviously, the sense of sight can well be said to constitute the most important factor in all understanding and learning processes. When all the foregoing is considered, it becomes clear that metaphors used in advertising posters as a form of visual product need be examined through semiotics.

In a research made on this topic in 2011, Çulha mentions that people have been in an effort to communicate with each other ever since they came into existence, and that therefore, when talking of signs we should not only address the words we speak or use in an article, but also visual elements. He also asserts that a sign can be in form of a poster, a graphic, a picture, a photo, smoke, cloud or symbols, or even a real object or event, and that the main purpose of all signs is to enable people to communicate with each other or with nature. (Çulha, 2011, p. 410). It is known that the first attempts of human beings to communicate with each other in their existence process did not start with writing but wall drawings to which they attached more than one meaning. As such, it is a historical fact that signs can be composed of not only text and words, but also with the help of images. After having addressed the concept of sign, it will be adequate identify next how to do semiotic analysis.

The sign, signified, and signifier constituting the basis of the theories of signs are of utmost importance for semiotic analysis (Çağlar quoting Atabek and Atabek, 2012, p. 27). To put it in more detail, in a study conducted in 2012, Çağlar defined the establishment of a relationship between the signifier and signified as "signification". For instance, seeing or hearing a signifier will make us envision its signified, i.e. the meaning of that signifier. Thus, the process of understanding begins, forming the basis of what can be gathered under the name of "signification" which contains in itself also the most important aspects of semiotic analysis, namely "denotation" and "connotation". For this process based on the theory of Roland Barthes, Barthes stated in his own evaluations (1976) that denotation refers to what a sign represents and connotation refers to how a sign is represented (Çağlar quoting Barthes, 2012, p. 26). Güvendi Kaptan asserted in 2017 that the importance of semiotics lies in the fact that it deals with signs and underlying meaning systems (Güvendi Kaptan, 2017, p. 1).

Semiotic methods and possibilities are employed with the aim of revealing how meanings are attributed to visualized messages and conveyed to the target audience in poster designs (Güvendi Kaptan, 2017, p. 2). The most significant reason why advertising posters are dealt with in this study from a semiotic point of view is that semiotic analysis is of great importance for understanding the message of an advertisement, as is also the case for posters. In a study performed in 2014, Yakın, Ay and Yakın put forth that a holistic analysis of advertisements can generally be possible by an evaluation of signs, denotations and connotations (Yakın, Ay and Yakın, 2014, p. 347).

In this study, advertising posters making use of verbal and visual metaphors were examined, along with an evaluation of these metaphors in terms of their manner of representation as well as the message they ascribe to the visual. This study comprising the evaluation of 5 different advertising posters was created based on the case study and interpretation methods, both being a qualitative research method.

1. Significance

Significance of this study is to examine the use of visual and verbal metaphors on posters, which are thought to be useful in designs by design and communication students and graphic and visual communication designers, to contribute to the literature in the light of the findings, and to inform designers, institutions and audiences about the subject.

2. Method and Data Analysis

This study was created based on the case study and interpretation methods, both being a qualitative research method.

> *"Case studies are a method to look at what is actually happening in real environment, to collect data systematically, to analyze and to reveal results. The resulting product is a sharp understanding of why an event is the way it is and what needs be focused on in more detail for future research."* (Aytaçlı quoting Davey (1991), 2012, p. 3).

> *"A philosophy, theory or art that tries to delve deeply into the meaning of a text, artistic product, behavior or a speaker's words is referred to as hermeneutics. Hermeneutics started to be used as a method of analysis in the field of qualitative research, based on the idea that since texts are interpretable a person's speech could be interpreted, too."* (Beisenbayeva quoting Karataş (2015), 2017, p. 65).

The examination part of this research involves the semiotic analysis of 5 metaphor-containing advertising posters retrieved from the internet and a discussion about their impact on purchase behaviors.

Image 1: *Mercedes (www.campaignsoftheworld.com)*

CONSUMER

	SIGN	SIGNIFIER	SIGNIFIED
VISUAL ELEMENT	Wrench	An image of a wrench used for repair	An image of a dinosaur shade placed behind the wrench, evoking a feeling of danger and fear
HEADER	Unofficial service can be dangerous	Written top left, i.e. the place which the eye first starts examining the poster design, in white color with a font size that suits visual hierarchy	Points out that vehicle repairs in unauthorized services can have very dangerous consequences
LOGO	Mercedes-Benz Logo	Written bottom right, i.e. the place which the eye sees last after having examined the poster design, in white color with a font size that suits visual hierarchy	Gives the message "this is what we think" by sharing the name and slogan of the company
BACKGROUND COLOR	Background in transitioning shades of grey	A dinosaur shade placed in the background	Association with fear, danger, and practices that may cause harm to the vehicle being repaired
MEANING OF THE VISUAL USED	Wrench	The wrench casting a shadow shaped like a dinosaur	Evoke the feelings of anxiety and fear while triggering archetypes of the subconscious through association with the likeliness of facing even larger problems if a vehicles is repaired by an unauthorized service or craftsman who lack adequate knowledge about the vehicle

Image 2: Ideal Bread (www.breadblog.net)

	SIGN	SIGNIFIER	SIGNIFIED
VISUAL ELEMENT	Bathroom scales	Image of a scales consisting of diet bread	Creates the impression that the bread, which is the product of the advertised brand, will have a minimal effect on the scale.
HEADER	No clear slogan visual	No slogan or header used, as not needed.	Absence of a slogan or header tries to reflect the company's sense of confidence in its product and itself.
LOGO	Ideal Logo	Seen on the advertised bread packaging in the bottom right, i.e. the place which the eye sees last after having examined the poster design.	While showing the company's name, it also wants to show the product packaging in order to tell which product it advertises.
BACKGROUND COLOR	Background in transitioning shades of red	Red background darkening from center to edges	Red is known as the color that stimulates appetite, triggers and encourages purchase.
MEANING OF THE VISUAL USED	Low-capacity bathroom scales	Image of a scales consisting of diet bread	Combination of a diet bread visual with a low-capacity bathroom scales gives the impression that the buyers of this product will attain weight control, while the red background is aimed at whetting the audience's appetite by giving the product a tasty image, thereby triggering in the audience the intention to purchase the product.

C O N S U M E R

Image 3: McDonald's (www.adsoftheworld.com)

	SIGN	SIGNIFIER	SIGNIFIED
VISUAL ELEMENT	Hamburger packaging of McDonald's	The hamburger packaging is resembled to a laptop computer.	A person using free Wi-Fi service while eating in a clean environment
HEADER	Free Wi-Fi served at all restaurants	Written right above the packaging and the poster's midpoint, in white color to increase legibility	Tells that people can use free Wi-Fi service at all of the brand's restaurants while eating their food there
LOGO	McDonald's Logo	Yellowish orange letter M on red background of the packaging	Since McDonald's is a well-known fast food company, the use of the letter M on a red background only is sufficient to create the desired association.
BACKGROUND COLOR	A plain and predominantly brown background to evoke the sense of a clean environment free of confusion.	Light background color in the center, getting darker towards the edges in order to focus the eye on the visual and slogan	The use of this background aims to point out the availability of not only a clean but also calm environment for internet use, while the brown color used for the restaurants' walls is aimed to create the image of quality.
MEANING OF THE VISUAL USED	Hamburger packaging and a customer reaching out	A computer image attributed to hamburger packaging	In order to rise to prominence in fierce competition environment, minimal use made of visuals to explain the service offered to customers in the most adequate way possible, while attributing the meaning of a laptop computer to hamburger packaging.

C O N S U M E R

Image 4: Doğanay Limonata (www. ideart.com.tr)

	SIGN	SIGNIFIER	SIGNIFIED
VISUAL ELEMENT	Image of a wooden hand fan with lemon slice pattern	Image of a lemon transformed into a hand fan	Hand fans have a cooling effect, here made of lemon and wood sticks both serving to highlight the product's naturalness.
HEADER	No clear slogan visual	The use of a logo in addition to product packaging has eliminated the need for a header or slogan	Use of a slogan or header found unnecessary based on the meaning attributed to the visual.
LOGO	Doğanay food logo	Seen on and right next to the advertised lemonade packaging in the bottom right, i.e. the place which the eye sees last after having examined the poster design.	Showing the packaging in addition to the company name in order to tell which product is being advertised, while creating association with naturalness by means of the leaved in logo.
BACKGROUND COLOR	Plain grey background highlighting the product	Grey background color, light in the center, getting darker towards the edges in order to focus the eye on the visual and make the visual come to the forefront	Highlighting the visual while giving the product a brighter appearance, thus creating a sense of freshness
MEANING OF THE VISUAL USED	Image of a wooden hand fan with lemon slice pattern	Image of a lemon transformed into a hand fan	It is aimed to create an image of freshness in summer heat by the use of vivid colors, sense of naturalness by the use of wood, a cooling effect by the use of a lemonade's visual, and the feeling of being energetic and happiness by the intense use of yellow.

C O N S U M E R

Image 5: Ford (www.yeniisfikirleri.net)

	SIGN	SIGNIFIER	SIGNIFIED
VISUAL ELEMENT	Car key	Urban skyline on the key	Creating the impression that you can reach every part of the city with the help of your car key.
HEADER	The city is in your hands	Written in white color for increased legibility, right above the urban skyline on the key where the background starts to shift from dark to light.	Tries to tell that thanks to your Ford car the whole city is in your hands and that you can easily reach every part of it.
LOGO	Ford Logo	Used both in the top left, i.e. the place which the eye first starts examining the poster design, and in the bottom right, i.e. the place which the eye sees last after having examined the poster design.	Used both at the start and end point when examining the poster so as to put emphasis on the brand. The aim is to achieve increased memorability.
BACKGROUND COLOR	Background in transitioning shades of blue	Blue background color, light in the center, getting darker towards the edges in order to focus the eye on the visual and core message	The blue background helps to support the brand's corporate colors while at the same time making reference to the air of the city. Blue also creates a sense of comfort and security and is in general a color that is used very commonly in technologic device advertisements.
MEANING OF THE VISUAL USED	Car key	Urban skyline on the key	Creating the image that having a Ford car will be sufficient to enjoy the city, by making use of an urban skyline on the key combined with the effects of visual, slogan and colors.

3. Conclusion

Ever since humanity came into existence, it made effort to communicate by attributing a wide range of meanings to visuals. Efforts to convey more information with less visuals date back to times as ancient as wall drawings. Later on, painters joined these efforts with their paintings. With the emergence of graphic design and visual communications, this method developed into a professional occupation as designers noticed that they received positive feedback when they conveyed their message to the target audience indirectly, rather than using straight-forward techniques. By the use of metaphors, connotative meanings can be attributed to visuals in addition to denotative meanings, thereby creating designs than can appeal to the feelings of the viewer and help to invigorate the viewer's subconscious.

A semiotic approach is adopted to analyze the designs created with the help of metaphors. For this reason, designers who will make use of metaphors in their designs and art directors or creative directors who will draw a road map for designers should have knowledge on the subject and be acquainted with semiotic analysis. Otherwise, they not only may fail to attribute the intended meanings to their design, but may cause attribution of meanings that could possibly be misunderstood and give rise to adverse consequences.

In conclusion, as can be seen also from the semiotic analyses made in this paper, posters making use of metaphors have been found to employ indirect ways to convey the intended message to the audience and that these posters are more likely to impress the target audience and trigger their purchasing intension by appealing to their subconscious when supported with slogans and visuals that involve allegories and concealed messages.

It is considered that metaphors used in posters which in this sense are believed to be different and more effective than others will make positive contribution both to attract the attention auf audience and to help designers create posters that convey a more effective message. Therefore, it is recommendable to include metaphors and semiotics into the curricula of courses associated with posters and advertising campaigns.

REFERENCES

Çobaner Ardıç, A. (2013). Sağlık iletişiminde korku öğesinin kullanımı: sigara paketlerinde kullanılan sigara karşıtı görsellerin göstergebilimsel analizi. İletişim Kuram ve Araştırma Dergisi, (37), 211 – 235.

Aytaçlı, B. (2012). Durum çalışmasına ayrıntılı bir bakış. Adnan Menderes Üniversitesi Eğitim Fakültesi Eğitim Bilimleri Dergisi, 3(1), 1-9.

Beisenbayeva, L., (2017) Türkiye Ve Kazakistan'da Eğitim Bilimleri Ve Alan Eğitimi Konusunda Lisansüstü Eğitimi Yapan Öğrencilerin Bilimsel Araştırma Yeterliklerinin İncelenmesi Gazi Üniversitesi Eğitim Bilimleri Enstitüsü Eğitim Programları Ve Öğretim Bilim Dalı Doktora Tezi, Ankara.

Ceylan, İ. G. ve Bahattin Ceylan, H. (2019), Reklam Tasarımlarında Tipografik Mizah Kullanımı Güzel Sanatlar Alaninda Araşırma Makaleleri (83 – 99) Ed. Dr.Öğr. Üyesi OKAN BOYDAŞ, Sonay ÖDEMİŞ, Ankara: Gece Kitaplığı.

Çağlar, B. (2012). Bir iletişim biçimi olarak göstergebilim. LAÜ Sosyal Bilimler Dergisi, 3(2), 22-34.

Çulha, O. (2012). Gösterge Bilim (Semiyotik) Tekniği Kullanıarak Kanada Fotoğraflarının İncelenmesi. Uluslararası Yönetim İktisat ve İşletme Dergisi, 7(13), 409-424.

Eraslan, L. (2011). Sosyolojik metaforlar. Akademik Bakış Dergisi, 27, 1-22.

Güvendi Kaptan, S. (2017) İletinin Görsel Tasarımlara Dönüştürülmesinde Göstergebilimsel Düşünme Süreçleri ve Cso İçin Afiş Uygulamaları Hacettepe Üniversitesi Güzel Sanatlar Enstitüsü Grafik Anasanat Dalı Sanatta Yeterlik Tezi, Ankara.

Yakın, V., Ay, C. ve Yakın, M. (2014) Reklamlarda Kullanılan Marka Kişilik Arketiplerinin Göstergebilimsel Analizi. Yönetim ve Ekonomi: Celal Bayar Üniversitesi İktisadi ve İdari Bilimler Fakültesi Dergisi, 21(1), 345-355.

Image Resources:

Image 1: Campaignsoftheworld (2015). [The dangers of unofficial service] Retrieved September,1, 2020, from https://i2.wp.com/campaignsoftheworld.com/wp-content/uploads/2015/02/mercedes_service_cotw_2.jpg?w=850&ssl=1

Image 2: Breadblog (2016) [Weight loss-Poor bread] Retrieved September,1, 2020, from https://mlo1n8w2nzhj.i.optimole.com/8N-MH3R0-egETG1jh/w:386/h:550/q:90/https://www.breadblog.net/wp-content/uploads/2016/08/ssss.jpg

Image 3: DDB Denmark Advertising Agency (2007-2008). McDonald's
Wi-Fi [Print advertisement poster]. Adsoftheworld. Retrieved September,1, 2020, from https://www.adsoftheworld.com/media/print/mcdonalds_wifi

Image 4: Ideart (n.d.) Doğanay Limonata [print advertisement poster] Retrieved September,1, 2020, from http://ideart.com.tr/assets/images/job/doganay-limonata.png

Image 5: Ogilvy (n.d.) Ford Fusion [Print advertisement poster]. Yeniisfikirleri. Retrieved September,1, 2020, from http://www.yeniisfikirleri.net/wp-content/uploads/2018/04/16-ford-fusion.jpg

CHAPTER 5

CURRENT TRENDS IN INTEGRATED MARKETING COMMUNICATION

Selçuk Yasin YILDIZ
Asst. Prof. Dr.
Sivas Cumhuriyet University, Turkey
selcukyasinyil@gmail.com
orcid.org/0000-0002-1594-8799

Abstract

As a result of important changes in marketing and communication technologies, modern marketing understanding has also changed. Communication in the center of modern marketing world activities. As a result, the necessity of marketing communication elements to work as a whole, in other words, the concept of integrated marketing communication has emerged in order to establish a more efficient communication. Among the new trends in integrated marketing communication used as social media marketing strategy; real-time marketing, interactive blogs, customer-based views and viral marketing concepts can be mentioned.

Keywords: *Marketing, Communication, Social Media, Consumer, Strategy*

Introduction

Increasing and stricter competition conditions, the increase in the knowledge level of consumers, and the advances in the consumers' access to information have necessitated businesses engaging in extensive marketing activities, and today the concept known as "integrated marketing communication" has emerged. It is thought that integrated marketing communication (IMC) can peak the communication activities that companies will implement to attract consumers and will help increase efficiency and productivity in marketing activities.

With the effect of developments in information technology, integrated marketing communication has been caused by the advent in marketing and marketing communication (Duncan & Everett, 1993). In another definition,

https://doi.org/10.2478/9788366675247-005

Kitchen and Burgmann (2010) expressed the integrated marketing communication as follows:

> *"Integrated marketing communication is a concept of marketing communications planning that recognizes the added value of a comprehensive plan that evaluates the strategic roles of a variety of communication disciplines (general advertising, direct response, sales promotion, and public relations) and combines these disciplines to provide clarity, consistency, and maximum communication impact."*

According to DeLozier (1976), marketing communication is the process of establishing effective communication with consumers by determining, interpreting, and acting according to the demands of the market to create the reactions that businesses want in their target group.

The importance of integrated marketing communication is remarkable in achieving the company goals effectively by carrying out all activities of the enterprises in coordination. In integrated marketing communication, instead of operating functions separately such as personal sales, advertising, public relations, and sales development, it is aimed to combine these components to serve the goals of the company as a whole (Schultz et al., 1993). With the help of integrated marketing communication, it is possible to reach the goals set by modern marketing more effectively (Dmitrijeva & Batraga, 2012).

According to the definitions of integrated marketing communication in the literature, it is seen that five main points draw attention. These points can be listed as follows (Kitchen & Burgmann, 2010):

    a. The exertion of communication ought to be directed towards consumers to influence behavior.
    b. An outside-in approach ought to be used; in other words, the customer should be the starting point while building a communication strategy.
    c. There should be a good relationship between the customer and the company.
    d. The contact points ought to contain all types of communication activities which is combined with the strategy in order to deliver the message correctly.
    e. There should be coordination between communication disciplines to create a competitive brand.

In integrated marketing communication, it is aimed to reach the target group effectively and efficiently and to create the necessary conditions for the efficiency of the aimed communication with the target group (De Pelsmacker et al., 2002). For this purpose, all communication marketing tools are used together in the integrated marketing communication to explain the company's targets to the target group in a persuasive and determined manner (Moriarty et al., 2017). In IMC, all marketing communication activities should be carried out in a disciplined, common, compatible, and integrated manner (Bozkurt, 2005).

The use of digitalization in every field, businesses turning towards commercial branding for differentiation, and globalization are some factors which are effective in the prominence of integrated marketing communication (Ivanov, 2012). As a result of the increase in globalization and the widespread use of digitalization with the effect of technological progress, it can be thought that companies tend to branding to gain competitive advantage. At this point, IMC is the key point in contributing to branding and increasing brand value for companies that want to gain a competitive advantage in local and global markets (Luxton et al., 2015). Because IMC refers to the process of planning, creating, integrating, and applying messages directly or indirectly towards a specific brand to influence the purchasing process (Stăncioiu et al., 2013).

The benefits of integrated marketing communication to companies are summarized by Kitchen and Burgmann (2010) as follows:

a. The approach of integrated marketing communication makes harmonized the short-and-long-term marketing to prevent conflicts in an organization,
b. Integrated marketing communication is a clear approach,
c. All target groups are taken into account in integrated marketing communication,
d. It should be encouraged that there is an individual and face-to-face communication with consumers
e. Creates a high synergy between all components subject to integrated marketing communication,
f. Provides overall financial benefits to the company.

1. The Components of Integrated Marketing Communication

According to Thorson, the basic components that make up the integrated marketing communication have been expressed as advertising, public relations, direct marketing, promotion, and packaging.

1.1. Advertising

Advertising is the game plan of statements and messages in time or space by companies, altruistic affiliations, government workplaces, and people hoping to enlighten just as persuade people from a particular target market or group as for their things, organizations, affiliations or musings (https://www.ama.org/topics/advertising/).

Advertising is characterized by the situation of declarations and alluring messages in time or space that are bought in broad communications. The reason of the elevating calling was to make ground-breaking messages and thereafter purchase space in expansive interchanges to contact a colossal group. Following this recipe, publicizing turned into an extremely viable showcasing correspondences strategy for well over a hundred years (Quesenberry, 2018).

Based on the definition made; To better understand the development of advertising, the three basic tasks of advertising can be explained as follows (Moriarty et al., 2017):

i. Identification: Advertising recognizes an item, the store where the item is sold, or both the item and the store. In its soonest years, publicizing zeroed in on recognizing an item and where you could get it. The absolute most punctual advertisements were essentially signing with the name or realistic picture of the kind of store, for example, shoemaker, merchant, or smithy.

ii. Information: Advertising gives data about an item. Advances in printing innovation toward the start of the Renaissance prodded education and got a blast of written words the type of banners, handbills, and papers. Education was not, at this point the identification of the world class, and it was conceivable to contact an overall crowd with more nitty gritty data about items.

iii. Persuasion: Advertising may convince individuals to purchase things. The Industrial Revolution quickened social change just as large-scale manufacturing. It brought the productivity of apparatus not exclusively to the creation of merchandise yet additionally to their dispersion. Effective creation in addition to more extensive appropriation implied that makers could offer a bigger number of items than their nearby business sectors could devour.

Publicizing has just been characterized as a paid and non-individual type of introduction and advancement of thoughts, products or administrations by a recognized supporter. In the light of this data, the points of advantages and disadvantages of promoting can be clarified as follows. Advantages of advertising (Khan, 2006):

i. It has low cost per contact.
ii. It can arrive at the clients where and when salesman cannot reach.
iii. It has incredible breadth for inventive versatility and performance of messages.
iv. Ability to make pictures which the sales rep can't. Inventive people are related with the item.
v. It has non-compromising nature of non-individual introduction.
vi. Advertising can possibly rehash the messages a few times.
vii. There is glory and grandness in Mass Media Advertising.

Despite these advantages, the disadvantages of advertising to companies are as follows:

i. It doesn't be able to bring the deals to a close.
ii. There is promoting mess i.e., an excessive number of commercial simultaneously.
iii. Customers regularly overlook the promoting messages.
iv. There is trouble in getting quick reaction or activity.
v. Inability to get criticism and to alter messages as wanted.
vi. There is trouble in estimating publicizing adequacy.
vii. It has generally high waste factor.

1.2. Public Relationship

Public relations are an unmistakable administration work, which builds up and keep up shared lines of correspondence, getting, acknowledgment and participation between an association and its publics; includes the administration of issues or issues; causes the executives to keep educated on and receptive to general assessment; characterizes and underlines the obligation of the board to serve the public intrigue; assists the executives with staying informed concerning and adequately use change, filling in as an early notice framework to help foresee patterns; and uses exploration and sound moral correspondence as its chief devices (Hutton, 1999).

It isn't vital, nonetheless, to remember a specific meaning of public relations. It's more imperative to recollect the catchphrases that are utilized in many definitions that outline the present current public relations. The catchphrases are (Wilcox et al., 2015):

Intentional (Public relations movement is purposeful. The intention of public relations is to impact, enhance understanding, give data, and take criticism from those affected by the movement.)

Arranged (Public relations movement is sorted out. Answers for issues are found and coordination are thoroughly considered, with the movement occurring over some undefined time frame. It is precise, requiring research and vital reasoning)

Execution (Compelling public relations depends on real strategies and execution. No measure of advertising will create altruism and backing if the association has helpless approaches and is inert to public concerns)

Public intrigue (Public relations movement ought to be commonly valuable to the association and the general population; it is simply the arrangement of the association's advantages with the public's interests and interests.)

Two-way correspondence (Public relations aren't simply scattering data yet in addition the craft of tuning in and participating in a discussion with different publics.)

The executives work (Public relations are best when it is a vital and indispensable piece of dynamic by top administration. Public relations include directing, critical thinking, and the administration of rivalry and struggle.)

Public relations are regularly mistaken for other correspondence-based controls, for example, showcasing, promoting, exposure and purposeful publicity, and it is additionally frequently misconstrued and abused. Just as being an incredible power for positive change, the inverse can likewise be valid and the term PR can, now and then reasonably, be utilized to portray activities that have been done to control or deceive. It is the devices and the aptitudes to utilize them that make it ground-breaking (Wolstenholme, 2013).

Collective to any far-reaching meaning of public relations are the accompanying components (Guth & Marsh, 2017):

i. Public relations are an administration work. The connection between an association and the publics imperative to its prosperity must be a top worry of the association's authority.

ii. Public relations include two-way correspondence. Correspondence isn't simply educating individuals regarding an association's needs. It likewise includes tuning in to those equivalent individuals discuss their interests. This ability to listen is a basic aspect of the relationship-building measure.

iii. Public relations are an arranged movement. Activities taken in the interest of an association must be deliberately arranged and predictable with the association's qualities and objectives. Furthermore, in light of the fact that the connection between an association and the publics imperative to its prosperity is a top concern, these activities should likewise be steady with the publics' qualities and objectives.

iv. Public relations are an examination-based sociology. Formal and casual exploration is directed to permit an association to convey successfully, having a full comprehension of the earth where it works and the issues it stands up to.

v. Public relations are socially capable. A professional's duties stretch out past authoritative objectives. Specialists and the individuals they speak to are required to assume a helpful part in the public eye.

Correspondences educator John Marston proposed a four-venture model dependent on explicit capacities: (i) Research, (ii) Action, (iii) Communication, and (iv) Evaluation. at whatever point a public relations proficient is confronted with a task—in the case of advancing a customer's item or safeguarding a customer's notoriety—the person ought to apply Marston's R-A-C-E approach (Seitel, 2017):

i. Research. Exploration perspectives about the current issue.

ii. Action. Distinguish activity of the customer in the public intrigue.

iii. Communication. Convey that activity to increase getting, acknowledgment, and backing.

iv. Evaluation. Assess the correspondence to check whether feeling has been affected.

1.3. Direct Marketing

Direct marketing is a specific specialty of the showcasing business. Like advertising, direct promoting includes investigating the necessities of an intended interest group and thinking about how best to configuration, bundle, and market an item or administration that addresses those issues (Basye, 2008).

Direct marketing is comprehensively characterized as a particular advancement of the advertising idea, which, with the assistance of current data and correspondence advances, places individualized client connections at the focal point of business exercises (Krafft et al., 2007).

From the decision-maker's perspective, the fundamental targets of direct marketing are as per the following; Getting new clients, building client steadfastness, improving client support, reacquiring lost clients, deals of items and administrations, marking and brand the board (Krafft et al., 2007).

Direct marketing utilizes media to convey a message that frequently requests that the shopper buy through a different, non-store dispersion channel by submitting an immediate request through a list or a site (Basye, 2008).

Through and through there are six fundamental achievement factors where the utilization of direct marketing is particularly significant (Krafft et al., 2007):

i. Responding to showcase patterns: market specialties; individualization; advancements in data innovation

ii. Predominance of client direction: client dedication; singular client connections

iii. Expanding adequacy: customization; creating more intrigue

iv. Requirement for adaptability: internationalization, in any event, for little spending plans; adaptable business

v. Precision in focusing on targets: decreased misfortunes because of selectivity; increasing expenses for other correspondence and deals power

vi. Execution of controlling: estimation of adequacy; count of benefit; testability

Skirting and around steps in building up an immediate direct marketing methodology results in come up short. Each progression gives data that improves and coordinates the system, via the outcome that great direct marketing causes more outcomes and less waste (Thomas et al., 2007):

i. Client Analysis: Profile your client's needs, inspiration, and purchasing profile. One should ask that ''What do they purchase and why?''

ii. Ecological Analysis: Companies need to foresee the inside requirements of their business in a proactive manner, yet additionally the following move of their opposition and rivalry that might develop.

iii. Serious Analysis: One should figure out what their adversaries are doing well and what they're fouling up. This will be a significant support for building up one's own message.

iv. Information Mining and Profiling: One should create an information base of possibilities, at that point remove and investigate however much appropriate data as could be expected to get the most ideal read on one's crowd.

v. Focusing on: One should further refine the information base to make sense of the best possibilities.

vi. Situating and Differentiating: One should develop the offer, or focal selling point, in a three-venture measure: (1) recognize the traits of the offer and the qualities that make it extraordinary from one's adversaries'; (2) outline the advantages the clients will endless supply of the offer; and, at last, (3) make guarantees that incorporate the guaranteed benefits for exploiting the offer.

vii. Special Value Proposition: One should shape the explanation that passes on a certain guarantee of an apparent worth; it will make them more attractive, more beneficial, wealthier, more astute, etc.

viii. Inventive Marketing Communications: One should decide how they'll form the message they've made. The message bundle contains every part of the standard mail crusade, including tone to the sort style to the source of inspiration.

ix. Direct Marketing Channels: One should figure out how they'll convey the message. Via mail? Pamphlet? Phone Call? One should pick an immediate showcasing channel which will best get their pitch into the hearts and brains of their clients.

x. Satisfaction and Service: Let's suppose that one's possibility chomps. How are they going to take care of her request or his solicitation for a free example or more data? One should ensure the satisfaction and administration tasks run easily and advantageously for their purchasers.

xi. Estimation and Assessment: One should track results so they get what they did well and what they did wrong. One's mission possibly worked on the off chance that it cost-viably crossed over the hindrance among you and your possibilities.

xii. Transformation and Innovation: One should revise, refine, and relaunch. In case they're not completely content with the consequences, they should not be hesitant to fiddle with the message, interchanges channel, or some other mission component.

1.4. Promotion

By definition, promotion refers to all promotional activities (except from advertising, public relations, personal selling, direct marketing, and online marketing/social media) that invigorate momentary conduct reactions from (1) purchasers, (2) the exchange (e.g., merchants, wholesalers, or retailers), or potentially (3) the organization's business power (Shimp & Andrews, 2013).

Promotion contains a scope of strategic promoting methods inside a vital advertising structure to enhance a product or service so as to accomplish explicit deals and marketing goals (Horchover, 2001). Promotion is viewed as an aspect of the entire showcasing exertion, making its commitment in a steady way to manufacture the brand or to drive benefit through deals (Mullin, 2010).

The primary goal of any promotion is to get somebody to purchase a product or service. Numerous advertisers utilize the AIDA idea to help achieve this objective. AIDA is an abbreviation that represents attention, interest, desire, and action, which are the four phases of promotion. Advancement must pull in the consideration of the customer, make an intrigue, transform the enthusiasm into a longing, and afterward convince the buyer to make a move (Kaser, 2013):

i. Attention: To sell a product or service, a business should initially catch the consideration of buyers and make mindfulness. This should be possible from various perspectives, for example, by utilizing intriguing visuals and incredible words. Sales reps can grab the eye of shoppers by utilizing an agreeable welcome. An advertising occasion, for example, a show supported by a business, is a decent method to make mindfulness.

ii. Interest: Product mindfulness doesn't generally prompt a deal. Advertisers must pick up the purchasers' advantage. Notices ought to convey the advantages of the item to tell individuals how might this benefit them in the event that they buy the item. Salesmen can give item shows to create intrigue.

iii. Desire: Interest and want are firmly related. As advertisers assemble enthusiasm for their item or administration, they should attempt to engage purchasers' purchasing thought processes (passionate, reasonable, and support). Salesmen can advance the wellbeing highlights of a vehicle to speak to families with youngsters. Café notices can show pictures of newly arranged burgers with all the fixings to tempt TV watchers.

iv. Action: Finally, advancements must persuade shoppers to take air behavior. A café may welcome clients to utilize a coupon on certain menu things. A retailer may advance limits on chosen stock. Salesmen can offer exceptional financing to assist customers with managing acquisition of extravagant things.

2. Current Trends in Integrated Marketing Communication

With the development of internet and information technologies, many disciplines are used in Marketing Communication today. Current trends used in integrated marketing communication can be listed as social media, neuromarketing and word-of-mouth marketing.

2.1. Social Media Marketing

The term social proposes two-route communications between individuals, which might be delegated coordinated, one-to-many, or many-to-many. Media, or devices that store and convey data, ordinarily incorporate materials that convey text, pictures, or sound, i.e., broad communications like books and magazines, TV, film, radio, and individual media like mail and phone (Hill et al., 2014).

Not, at this point happy with advertising and promotional data as a mere hotspot for discovering new items and administrations, buyers have taken to the Social Web with an ultimate objective to share among themselves their own prompt encounters with brands, items, and services to give a more "genuine" perspective on their exploration experience (Evans & McKee, 2010).

Social media is the democratization of data, changing individuals from content peruses into content distributers. Social media utilizes the "insight of groups" to interface data in a community way. Social media can take a wide range of structures, including Internet gatherings, message sheets, weblogs, wikis, webcasts, pictures and video.Instances of social media applications are Google, Wikipedia, My-Space, Facebook, Last.fm, YouTube, Second Life, and Flickr (Evans, 2008).

The expression social media marketing by and large alludes to utilizing these online services for relationship selling — a subject you definitely thoroughly understand. Social media administrations or channels utilize new online innovations to achieve recognizable correspondence and showcasing objectives. All that you definitely think about promoting is right. Social media marketing is another method, not another world (Zimmerman & Sahlin, 2010).

Social media marketing conveys numerous advantages. One of the majorities of significant is that you don't need to front any money for most administrations. Obviously, there's a drawback: Most administrations require a noteworthy speculation of time to start and keep up asocial media promoting effort (Zimmerman & Sahlin, 2010).

It can be said that there are five essential preferences to be effective in this field in order to understand the advantages of social media marketing (Nadaraja & Yazdanifard, 2013):

    i. Cost-related: When contrasted with others, budget related impediments to social media marketing are quite low. The majority of social media locales are permitted to get the chance to, create profile and post information. Customary marketing attempts can cost lots of dollars, but various social media devices are free in any case, for business use.

    ii. Social Interaction: The fact that it has expanded and created new types of social communication is one of the well-known phenomena of recent media. Customer behavior examines uncover that people offer more prominent thought to guidance and data shared web based, investing more energy with sites that give outsider assessments.

iii. Interactivity: Interactivity is regarded as one of the identifying features of new media developments; it gives more remarkable admittance to data similarly as supporting extended customer control and commitment to social media content.

iv. Targeted market: Social media provide advertisers the ability to target groups and shoppers dependent website the vicinity clients' very own advantages and what their companions like.

v. Customer Service: Customer assistance is another crucial part of social media marketing. At times web specialists can't stay away from a specific level of multifaceted nature in the engineering of a site. Hence, it is important to have an insightful customer support framework.

2.2. Neuromarketing

Neuromarketing is hence kind of a merger of neuroscience and marketing, which empowers progress in the information on how individuals settle on choices and by what method would marketers be able to impact these choices. Neuromarketing can be shortsightedly characterized as another zone of marketingthat tries to reveal the effect of marketing boosts on the responses of clients and buyers simultaneously when settling on buying choices (Horská & Berčík, 2017).

Marketing is a field given to affecting individuals to like things, and at last to purchase things, including things they may not require. Marketers know that individuals have cerebrums. Marketing, thusly, is currently and consistently has been committed to impacting cerebrums. Neuromarketing is another approach to quantify whether and how marketing is functioning. Neuromarketers trust it's a superior method to quantify promoting on the grounds that it depends on a more practical comprehension of how consumers' brains work (Genco et al., 2013).

Foreseeing consumer behavior has consistently been a significant enthusiasm of marketing specialists. Conventional showcasing explores are as yet successful and will be utilized in promoting. Be that as it may, there are circumstances when it is important to supplement regular techniques by current ones. Marketing specialists state that advertisers will never again be guided by what the respondents pronounce about themselves in overviews, on the grounds that their brain – the part that doesn't imagine anything – frequently repudiates it (Horská & Berčík, 2017).

Taking this wide perspective on neuromarketing, there are three significant ways that it can assist us with bettering get marketing and consumer behavior (Genco et al., 2013):

    i. It can mention to us what's happening in individuals' brains while they are encountering a marketing boost.

    ii. It can disclose to us how brains respond to marketing improvements introduced in various situational settings.

    iii. It can reveal to us how brains make an interpretation of those responses into shopper choices and practices.

2.3. Word-of-mouth Marketing

Word-of-mouthmarketing (WOM) is the cycle of data trade, particularly proposals about items and administrations, between two individuals in a casual way (O'Leary & Sheehan, 2008).Word-of-mouth marketing, to summarize briefly, is verbal advertising or oral communication.

The definition comprises of three fundamental parts. To begin with, word-of-mouth is relational communication. This component separates word-of-mouth from mass correspondence and other generic channels accessible for buyers. Second, the substance of word-of-mouth from an advertising viewpoint is business. The message is about business substances, items, item classifications, brands and marketers or even their advertising. Third, despite the fact that the substance of word-of-mouth is business, the communicators are not spurred economically, or possibly they are seen not to be. They don't discuss brands since they are workers of the organization, or get any motivators from it (Kirby & Marsden, 2006).

In numerous business sectors, clients are firmly impacted by the assessments of their friends. Word-of-mouth marketing alludes to marketing procedures that use the clients' informal organizations to build brand mindfulness through self-replication and message dispersion. The clients' interpersonal organizations would influence the selection of individual advancements and items and lessen the danger of customers' buying dynamic. Online client audits would impact other clients' impression of item and could be considered as a feature of the word-of-mouth marketing. Estimating the compelling intensity of the commentators is basic in word-of-mouth marketing in light of the fact that the evaluated powerful quality can be utilized to find the hubs generally proper for spreading item data rapidly, broadly, and viably (Y.-M. Li et al., 2010).

Two different word-of-mouth marketing are mentioned in the literature, positive and negative word-of-mouth marketing. Positive WOM happens when clients happy with an item or administration share about it with others (Buttle, 1998). Negative WOM is a buyer reaction to disappointment with an item or administration (Richins, 1984). Word-of-mouth marketingis a sort of viral marketingand a casual method of trading data among buyers about the qualities, use, and responsibility for items or administrations. It shifts correspondence from an organization to-client mode to a clienttoclient mode. Word-of-mouth marketinghas more grounded noteworthiness than different types of marketing, as there is no immediate association between the data sender and the dealer, and in this way the data given is viewed as emotional and free. It might likewise be more influential, as the data sender may have a superior comprehension of the collector (F. Li & Du, 2011).

Conclusion

Until recently, companies have run their marketing communication activities by different units. Despite the costs incurred for different units, the companies could not communicate with consumers at the desired level. This situation led the companies to various kinds of searches and helped the emergence of integrated marketing communication. Integrated marketing communication is a marketing process that takes place by combining all sales and communication opportunities of the company with other marketing mix elements.

Until today, integrated marketing mix has included advertising, public relations, personal sales, direct marketing, sales development, sponsorship, fair organization, e-marketing, packaging, goal marketing, word-of-mouth marketing, and event marketing components. In the future, digital marketing components such as social media marketing, neuromarketing, and e-word-of-mouth marketing are expected to be integrated.

Current trends used in integrated marketing communication are mentioned by means of this study. In addition to the components mentioned, digital marketing-based components can also play an active role in integrated marketing communication. Marketing communication professionals' use of integrated marketing communications and digital marketing can contribute to the field of marketing.

REFERENCES

Basye, A. (2008). Opportunities in direct marketing. McGraw-Hill.

Bozkurt, İ. (2005). Bütünleşik pazarlama iletişimi. MediaCat.

Buttle, F. A. (1998). Word of mouth: Understanding and managing referral marketing. Journal of Strategic Marketing, 6(3), 241–254.

De Pelsmacker, P., Geuens, M., & Anckaert, P. (2002). Media context and advertising effectiveness: The role of context appreciation and context/ad similarity. Journal of Advertising, 31(2), 49–61.

DeLozier, M. W. (1976). Marketing communications process. McGraw-Hill.

Dmitrijeva, K., & Batraga, A. (2012). Barriers to integrated marketing communications: The case of Latvia (small markets). Procedia-Social and Behavioral Sciences, 58, 1018–1026.

Duncan, T. R., & Everett, S. E. N. V.-3. (1993). Client perceptions of integrated marketing communications . Journal of Advertising Research, 32, 30–39.

Evans, D. (2008). Social media marketing: An hour a day. Wiley Publishing, Inc.

Evans, D., & McKee, J. (2010). Social media marketing: The next generation of business engagement. Wiley Publishing, Inc.

Genco, S. J., Pohlmann, A. P., & Steidl, P. (2013). Neuromarketing for dummies. John Wiley & Sons.

Guth, D. W., & Marsh, C. (2017). Public relations : A values-driven approach (Sixth). Pearson.

Hill, C. A., Dean, E., & Murphy, J. (2014). Social media, sociality, and survey research. John Wiley & Sons, Inc.

Horchover, D. (2001). Sales Promotion. Capstone Publishing.

Horská, E., & Berčík, J. (2017). Neuromarketing in food retailing. Wageningen Academic Publishers.

Hutton, J. G. (1999). The definition, dimensions, and domain of public relations. Public Relations Review, 25(2), 199–214.

Ivanov, A. E. (2012). The internet's impact on integrated marketing communication. Procedia Economics and Finance, 3, 536–542.

Kaser, K. (2013). Advertising & Sales Promotion. South-Western, Cengage Learning.

Khan, M. (2006). Consumer behaviour and advertising management. New Age International (P) Limited.

Kirby, J., & Marsden, P. (2006). Connected marketing: The viral, buzz and word-of-mouth revolution. Butterworth-Heinemann.

Kitchen, P. J., & Burgmann, I. (2010). Integrated marketing communication. In J. N. Sheth &N. K. Malhotra (Eds.), Wiley international encyclopedia of marketing. John Wiley & Sons Ltd .

Krafft, M., Hesse, J., Höfling, J., Peters, K., & Rinas, D. (2007). International direct marketing: Principles, best practices, marketing facts. Pearson.

Li, F., & Du, T. C. (2011). Who is talking? An ontology-based opinion leader identification framework for word-of-mouth marketing in online social blogs. Decision Support Systems2, 51(1), 190–197.

Li, Y.-M., Lin, C.-H., & Lai, C.-Y. (2010). Identifying influential reviewers for word-of-mouth marketing. Electronic Commerce Research and Applications, 9(4), 294–304.

Luxton, S., Reid, M., & Mavondo, F. (2015). Integrated marketing communication capability and brand performance. Journal of Advertising, 44(1), 37–46.

Moriarty, S., Mitchell, N., Wood, C., & Wells, W. (2017). Advertising & IMC: Principle & Practice (Eleventh). Pearson.

Mullin, R. (2010). Sales promotion: How to create, implement & integrate campaigns that really work (Fifth). Kogan Page Limited.

Nadaraja, R., & Yazdanifard, R. (2013). Social media marketing: Advantages and disadvantages.

O'Leary, S., & Sheehan, K. (2008). Building buzz to beat the big boys : Word-of-mouth marketing for small businesses. Praeger Publishers.

Quesenberry, K. A. (2018). Social media strategy : Marketing, advertising, and public relations in the consumer revolution (Second). Rowman & Littlefield.

Richins, M. L. (1984). Word of mouth communication as negative information. NA - Advances in Consumer Research, 11, 697–702.

Schultz, D. E., Tannenbaum, S., & Lauterborn, R. (1993). Integrated marketing communications. Lincolnvvood: NTC Business Book.

Seitel, F. P. (2017). The practice of public relations (Thirteenth). Pearson.

Shimp, T. A., & Andrews, J. C. (2013). Advertising, Promotion, and other aspects of Integrated Marketing Communications. Cengage Learning.

Stăncioiu, A.-F., Botoș, A., Orzan, M., Pârgaru, I., & Arsene, O. (2013). Integrated marketing communication in tourism–an analysis. Case study: Muntenia and Oltenia. Theoretical and Applied Economics, 20(6), 7–34.

Thomas, A. R., Lewison, D. M., Hauser, W. J., & Foley, L. M. (2007). Direct marketing in action : Cutting-edge strategies for finding and keeping the best customers. Praeger Publishers.

Wilcox, D. L., Cameron, G. T., & Reber, B. H. (2015). Public relations: Strategies and tactics (11th ed.). Pearson.

Wolstenholme, S. (2013). What public relations is and what it is not. In S. Wolstenholme (Ed.), Introduction to Public Relations. Pearson.

Zimmerman, J., & Sahlin, D. (2010). Social media marketing all-in-one for Dummies. Wiley Publishing, Inc.

CHAPTER 6

THE ROLE OF SMART PACKAGING IN COMMUNICATING WITH THE CONSUMER

Hatice BAHATTİN CEYLAN
Lecturer
Sinop University, Gerze Vocational School, Department of Design
hbahattin@sinop.edu.tr
orcid.org/0000-0002-4528-5180

Abstract

With the increasing product range and the conscious consumer group which makes preferences and comparisons, and keeps its expectations high, the packaging sector also changes over time and embraces many innovations. The smart packaging, integrated with the technology, has been slowly replacing the traditional and static packaging. These packaging technologies are in the position of a sales representative that is in communication with the consumers and that directs the consumers, provides information about the product and is in interaction with the target audience rather than merely being a design accessory of the packaging. In this study, the technological accessories that provide an innovative approach to the design of the packaging in the digital environment such as time/temperature indicators, NFC labels and QR codes, are examined and the differences are evaluated in terms of their ease of use, affordability and the contributions that they provide to the customer.

Keywords: *Communication Design, Consumer Behavior, Packaging Technology, Smart Packaging.*

Introduction

While nowadays countless product types for different target groups are produced, companies strive to make their products visible to buyers. In contrast to the spiral of the past which used to have a protective function only, enhancing a product's visibility on a platform as complex as this requires now a packaging that functions as a seller to market the product and make it communicate with the consumer. According to Becer (2014), several studies have shown that consumers make their purchasing decisions by looking at the packaging, not the content of the product. Therefore, packaging should

https://doi.org/10.2478/9788366675247-006

capable to tell the consumer something about the product in the shortest time possible (Becer, 2014, p. 15). Along with packaging graphic design, other factors important in terms of design include the industrial structure of packaging, the materials used, and even the messages ascribed thereto (Ceylan and Ceylan, 2015, p. 139), because efficient marketing of any product offered for sale calls for packaging that can positively differentiate the product from its peers. As a result, smart packaging has started to replace traditional packaging with each passing day. The use of technological innovations along with the color, typography and illustration of packaging are closely associated with a product's quality perception. Hence, the interaction established between packaging capable to effectively market a product to consumers and today's technology excites attention among customers and makes them decide in favor of this type of packaging when buying a product. In their publications, Schaefer and Cheung (2018) stated that the global market for smart packaging, which also serve to protect both the consumer and product, will reach $ 26.7 billion by 2024 (Schaefer and Cheung, 2018, p. 1022). Indicators integrated into packaging of consumer products like food and pharmaceuticals provide the consumer with quick information on the reliability and freshness of the product and also protect them against possible food/drug poisoning.

The purpose of this research paper is to examine and reveal the ways in which technological add-ons such as barcodes, RFID tags and packaging indicators are recently being used by the packaging industry in the design of various packaging, and also how and to what extent smart packaging equipped with these innovations contribute to product sales and consumer satisfaction.

1. Methodology and Limitations

The scanning model was employed for the literature research section of this research paper prepared to show that various technological add-ons capable of communicating with the consumer are used on packaging and to assert the positive and/or adverse effects thereof on the consumer as well as the contributions they make to the sector. A literature review was performed to investigate the smart packaging that form the basis of this research and the effects thereof on the consumer, while visuals were used to support the information obtained. Besides, a smart packaging of the brand "Rémy Martin" capable to communicate with the consumer was taken as example to analyze the impact of smart packaging on the consumer. This study is limited to available literature sources, 6 smart packaging tools and 1 smart packaging visual used during analysis.

2. Communication of Packaging with the Consumer & Smart Packaging

The purpose of packaging food is to protect the product from chemical and microbial contamination and environmental factors such as light, oxygen and water vapor. While packaging in this form is inactive, the idea of active and smart packaging has attracted much more attention in recent years and has been used by many trademarks (Otles and Yalcin, 2008, p. 1). Smart packaging provide both the consumer and producer with information on the quality, benefit and safety of the product and ensure that early action can be taken, as necessary. According to Chen et al. (2020), smart packaging technologies can transfer accurate data about the status of products and help to reduce food loss and waste, while also protecting the brand (Chen et al., 2020, p. 523).

Kocaman and Sarımehmetoğlu (2010) defined the following 6 categories for smart packaging tools:

1. Barcodes and Radio-Frequency Identification (RFID) Tags
2. Time/Temperature Indicators (TTIs)
3. Gaz Sensors / Indicators
4. Biosensors
5. Nanosensors
6. Freshness Indicators

The following section provides general information on the definition and functioning of these tools used on product packaging;

Linear Barcode, QR Code and Radio-Frequency Identification (RFID) Tags:
Also referred to as information coding technology, barcodes are machine-readable interfaces that give access to coded data through the use of optical readers. The most common type today is linear barcodes. While linear barcodes can code 20 alphanumerical characters, this number can be as high as 4000 in QR Codes. (Acartürk, 2012, p. 117).

Image 1: *Linear barcode (left) and QR code (right)*

This opportunity provided by QR Code technology has put packaging into a position where they assume the role of the marketer communicating with the consumer and providing the consumer with full-detailed information about the product. In today's world where internet shopping in an ever-increasing trend, consumers want to be able to experience advanced technology also in real shopping environment. Thanks to this technology, consumers do not only get a comprehensive idea about the product, but also have access to recipes of meals that they can cook with the product they purchase, giveaways and entertaining videos, thus getting into a positive interaction with the product (Image 2).

Image 2: *Packaging with a QR code*

While this technology was not a suitable option for visually impaired people until recently, these people can now easily listen the message on their smart phones, with the help of dedicated mobile apps such as voice QR code, barrier-free tag or Voiceye code (Image 3).

Image 3: *Packaging with a voice QR code*

Radio-Frequency Identification (RFID) tags, on the other hand, are superior to barcodes or manual systems as they are readable without the need for contact or visual focusing. RFID tags are intelligent electronic information-based packaging add-ons that use radio frequency electromagnetic fields to transfer data (Akkemik & Güner, 2020, p. 14). Although they may function in different ways, RFID tags serve similar purposes as those of other smart packaging systems. Likewise, RFID tags do also help the consumer to obtain information about the product, while helping the packaging to fulfill its function of protecting both the product and the consumer. The disadvantage of RFID tags is their high cost.

Image 4: Radio-frequency identification (RFID) tag

NFC tags are a subcategory of RFID tags, but they are more complex and more equipped. Consumers having an NFC-enabled phone can make contactless payment via radio waves. NFC tags are capable of two-way communication. However, as NFC is a close-distance communication technology, its use is limited to distances up to 5 cm max. (acod.com). Today, there are a wide range of brands that make use of NFC technology in their packaging designs to actively communicate with their consumers (Image 5).

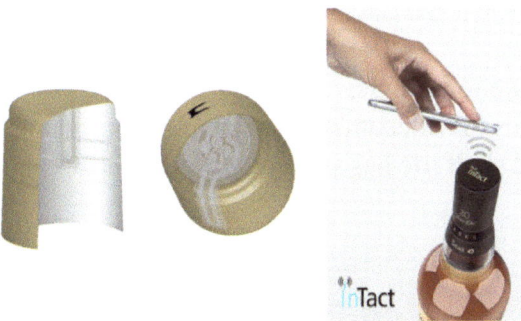

Image 5: Positioning and use of an NFC tag

Time Temperature Tags:

TTIs are a self-adhesive label system that make use of color changes on the label to inform the consumer on certain chemical, mechanical or microbial deterioration of the product as a result of exposure to temperature. TTI labels are usually designed to alert when a pre-determined temperature is exceeded during transport or storage of frozen food and can be classified in 3 subgroups, namely polymer, diffusion and enzymatic-based tags. (Özçandır and Yetim, 2010, p. 3).

Image 6: *Time/Temperature Indicator (TTI) tag*

Advantages of TTI labels are low cost and easy positioning on the packaging material. Another opportunity made available by this technology is the chance to get the "first in first out" (FIFO) or "last in last out" (LILO) strategies replaced by shelf-life modelling, i.e. the "first expired first out" (FEFO) method. (Hepsağ and Varol, 2018, p. 34).

TTIs bring several benefits for the consumer, namely they:

• ensure that consumers consume healthy and safe products in terms of nutritional value and health compatibility,
• are an understandable and interesting tool for the consumer,
• contain clear messages for companies thanks to their customizable design,
• contribute to savings,
• motivates the consumer to consume the products before they expire once their second shelf life has started, i.e. after unpacking the product (sedef.com).

Gaz Sensors / Indicators:

These are sensors used to measure the composition of gas in the packaging of products with a vacuum packaging or MAP (Modified Atmosphere Packaging). They can also be used to get an idea about the quantity of gas in the contents of a packaging or in food storage rooms. Fluorescent-based sensors are also used to identify the quantity of gas formed in the gap at the top of food. When the amount of oxygen in food packaging reaches the polymer that contains fluorescent or fluorescent dye, it causes the material of packing to sparkle (dunyagida.com / Güleç, 2017).

Biosensors:

Biosensors are used to sense the reactions that may occur in packaged products and identify any reaction-related alterations resulting from spoilage of the product. There are a large variety of biosensors, while selection of a given biosensor type is made according to the compound that is released when spoilage occurs (Öcal and Karapınar, 2016, p. 449).

Nanosensors:

Nanosensors in smart packaging are used for early detection of food spoilage and to prevent the consumption of spoiled food. China and the United States are the countries that show highest interest in nanotechnology, followed by Japan and European countries. In our country, the National Nanotechnology Research Center (UNAM) established under the roof of Bilkent University by decision of the State Planning Organization is the first center to focus on nanotechnologies. (Süfer and Karakaya, 2011, p. 87-88).

Freshness Indicators:

Freshness indicators are smart packaging labels that change color as a result of microbial spoilage. This type of indicators are very sensitive and product specific (Lechuga (2006) as quoted by Satouf and Köten, 2019). Freshness indicators are mostly seen on the packaging of fresh vegetables, fruits or meat and fish products. This smart packaging application serves the same purposes within the scope of consumer and product protection as other labels and indicators.

Thanks to this add-on, consumers can easily see the information about the product's packaging time and remaining shelf life by looking at the color changes on the label (Yayan & Ceylan, 2018, p. 874). Firms that sell fresher products instead of products approaching their expiry will contribute to the reliability of their brand in the eyes of the consumer by adopting an ethical sales strategy.

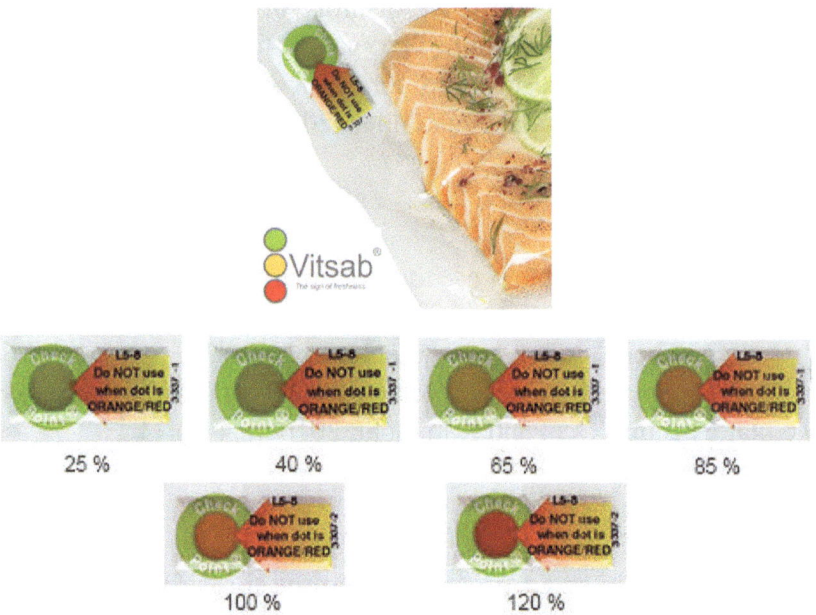

Image 7: *Freshness indicator on fish packaging*

In the following section of this paper, an image of a smart packaging of the brand "Rémy Martin", limited to the NFC label, that is thought to leave a positive impression on the consumer is taken as example to analyze the possible impacts of smart packaging on the brand, product reliability and the consumer.

3. Analysis: NFC Impacts of "Rémy Martin"

Notable for its flamboyant bottle design (Image 8), Rémy Martin, a French brand that was founded in 1724 and produces cognac, is a member of Comité Colbert. Founded in 1954, the Comité Colbert brings together famous brands and promotes luxury.

Image 8: Rémy Martin's X.O. Excellence and Extra Bottles

The brand's products are put on the market in diamond cut bottles with metallized labels and gilded printed cardboard packaging, which is closely associated with the brand's efforts to gain the admiration of the consumer, increase product reliability and establish an emotional bond with the consumer to make them develop and exhibit a positive attitude towards the brand.

Image 9: Rémy Martin Remy Martin Cognac Louis XIII Bottle

When the products are examined, it can be seen that the brand took initiative in 2015 and replaced its traditional packaging style with a smart packaging strategy (Image 10). Launched on the company's official website as "Rémy Martin's Connected Bottle", this bottle is described to be capable of communicating with the consumer directly thanks to high security NFC tag, and to have several advanced functions such as providing secure authentication, highly secure opening detection technology, access to an integrated game & rewards program.

Image 10: "NFC Labelled" Rémy Martin Bottle

Thanks to this small NFC tag placed under the bottle cap, the consumer can instantly access manifold information about the product, thus creating consumer loyalty towards the brand.

4. Conclusion and Suggestions

In this research, we examined the smart packaging tools and explained their functioning, usage areas and positive/adverse impacts they create on the consumer. The never-ending struggle to attract the consumers' attention among a vast range of countless products causes companies to constantly renew their packaging and develop effective strategies. Today, due to this concern, traditional packaging has begun to get replaced by smart packaging more and more. RFID tags, QR codes that can fit up to 4000 alphanumeric characters, sensors that can pre-sense the product's release of harmful gases, fluorescent-based sensors that cause the package to sparkle when the presence of these gases is detected, and indicators that enable consumers to easily see the packaging and expiry dates of frozen food by means of color changes are all leaving a positive effect on the consumer and instill trust towards the brand. Thanks to this technology capable to provide instant response to questions which the consumer may have in his mind when taking a product in hand, the consumer gets the chance to see the freshness of the product, whether it was opened before, and whether a microbial interaction has occurred. In addition, special "voice QR codes" have been developed for visually impaired people so that these people too can make use of these tools put at the disposal of consumers.

It can be seen that luxury brands trying to meet consumer expectations at a high level are also opting for smart packaging. When the packaging applied by the famous brand "Rémy Martin", it was seen that they combines quality and luxury with smart packaging technology. Thanks to high security NFC tag placed under the bottle cap, the customer gets instant access to secure authentication, highly secure opening detection technology, and an integrated game & rewards program.

Based on these results, it is an important gain for the sector if and when companies and packaging designers closely follow technological developments and have an idea about the use of these technological add-ons in packaging. Hence, it is recommended that the packaging designs to be created henceforward should make use of these technologies, with full awareness of the positive impact that smart packaging tools will make on both the consumer and brand.

REFERENCES

Acartürk, C. (2012). Barkod teknolojilerinin eğitimde kullanımı: Bilişsel bilimler çerçevesinde bir değerlendirme. Akademik Bilişim'12-XIV. Akademik Bilişim Konferansı Bildirileri, 117-122.

Akkemik, Y., & Güner, A. (2020). Gıda Ambalaj Sistemlerinde Yeni Yaklaşımlar: Akıllı Ambalaj Sistemleri. Türk Bilimsel Derlemeler Dergisi, 13(1), 9-22.

Becer, E. (2014). Ambalaj tasarımı. Ankara: Dost Kitabevi Yayınları.

Ceylan, İ. G., & Ceylan, H. B. (2015). Ambalaj Tasariminda Bilinçalti Mesaj Öğelerinin ve Nöropazarlama Yaklaşiminin Kullanimlarinin Karşılaştırılması. Electronic Turkish Studies, 10(2). 123-142.

Chen, S., Brahma, S., Mackay, J., Cao, C., & Aliakbarian, B. (2020). The role of smart packaging system in food supply chain. Journal of Food Science, 85(3), 517-525.

Hepsağ, F., Varol, T. (2018). Intelligent Packaging Use In Food Industry And Traceability, The Journal of ADYUTAYAM 6(1), 29-39.

Kocaman, N., & Sarımehmetoğlu, B. (2010). Gıdalarda akıllı ambalaj kullanımı. Veteriner Hekimler Derneği Dergisi, 81(2), 67-72.

Otles, S., & Yalcin, B. (2008). Intelligent food packaging. LogForum 4, 4, 3. 1-9

Öcal, D., Karapınar, D. Ç. (2016). Reflections of Packaging System To Consumers 5th International Printing Techologies Symposium, 445-454.

Özçandır, S., & Yetim, H. (2010). Akıllı ambalajlama teknolojisi ve gıdalarda izlenebilirlik. Electronic Journal of Food Technologies, 5(1), 1-11.

Satouf, M., & Köten, M. Gıda Üretim Sektöründe Kullanılan Ambalajlara Genel Bir Bakış. 3. International Conference on Agricultre, Food, Veterinary and Pharmacy Sciences.

Schaefer, D., & Cheung, W. M. (2018). Smart packaging: opportunities and challenges. Procedia CIRP, 72, 1022-1027.

Süfer, Ö., & Karakaya, S. (2011). Gıda endüstrisi ve nanoteknoloji: durum tespiti ve gelecek. Akademik Gıda, 9(6), 81-88.

Yayan, G., & Ceylan, H. B. (2018). Ambalaj Tasarımında İnteraktif Yaklaşımlar ve Tasarım Öğrencilerinin Konu Hakkındaki Farkındalığının Ölçülmesi. İdil Sanat ve Dil Dergisi, 7(47), 873-879.

Internet Resources:

Güleç H. A. (2017, 13 April). Latest trends in food packaging, Dünya-Gıda E-Journal Retrieved October, 2, 2020, from http://www.dunyagida.com.tr/haber/gida-ambalajlarinda-son-trendler/6532

Şahbaz, Y.(2018, 6 October).Görme engelliler için engelsiz etiket, Anadolu Agency Retrieved October, 2, 2020, from https://www.aa.com.tr/tr/turkiye/gorme-engelliler-icin-engelsiz-etiket/1274191

Voiceye Görme Engelliler İçin Karekod Sistemi (n.d) Beyid Retrieved October, 2, 2020, from https://www.beyid.com.tr/3125-2/

Nfc ve Rfid (2015) Boer Bilişim AŞ Retrieved October, 2, 2020, from https://www.acod.com.tr/makale_detay.asp?id=8

İzler Sıcaklık Zaman Etiketleri (n.d.) Sedef Retrieved October, 2, 2020, from http://www.sedef.com/izler_sicaklik_zaman_etiket.php

Image Resources:

Image 1: Pazarlamaturkiye - Gözütok, Ö. (2019) Karekod Nedir ve Nasıl Kullanılmaz? [Qr Code] Retrieved October, 2, 2020, from https://pazarlamaturkiye.com/wp-content/uploads/2019/07/karekod-nedir-nas%-C4%B1l-kullanilmaz.jpeg
Gepir (n.d.) Barkod Numarası (GTIN) İle Arama [Linear barcode] Retrieved October, 2, 2020, from http://gepir.org.tr/images/gtin6.jpg

Image 2: Dollard-packaging (n.d.) [QR pic 1] Retrieved October, 2, 2020, from https://www.dollard-packaging.ie/wp-content/uploads/2018/04/QR-pic-1.jpg

Image 3: Anadolu Ajansı – Şahbaz, Y., Mengüarslan, E. (2018) Görme engelliler için engelsiz etiket [Packaging with a voice QR code Photograph] Retrieved October, 2, 2020, from https://www.aa.com.tr/tr/turkiye/gorme-engelliler-icin-engelsiz-etiket/1274191

Image 4: Advantechindia.com (n.d.) [RFID Label] Retrieved October, 2, 2020, from https://5.imimg.com/data5/EH/QI/MY-2551700/rfid-250x250.jpg

Image 5: Amazonaws.com - Packagingnews.com.au, Nelson, J. (2019) Amcor Toppan bring out NFC wine capsule [NFC Tag] Retrieved October, 2, 2020, from https://yaffa-cdn.s3.amazonaws.com/yaffadsp/images/dmImage/StandardImage/intact_image1.png

Image 6: Sedef (n.d.) İzler Sıcaklık Zaman Etiketleri [Time/Temperature Indicator (TTI) tag] Retrieved October, 2, 2020, from http://www.sedef.com/image_slide/img/izler_altsayfa_TTI1.jpg

Image 7: Fis (2014) Vitsab, the Sign of Freshness [Freshness indicator on fish packaging] Retrieved October, 2, 2020, from https://fis.com/fis/techno/photolib/47042_300x300_72_DPI_0.jpg

Image 8: Licorea (n.d.) [Remy Martin X.O. Excellence Package] Retrieved October, 2, 2020, from https://www.licorea.com/remy-martin-xo-excellence-p-525.html?language=en
Wnfdiary (2019) [Remy Martin Extra Bottles] Retrieved October, 2, 2020, from https://wnfdiary.com/wp-content/uploads/2019/04/remy-martin-extra-fine-champagne-cognac.jpg

Image 9: Wallywine (n.d.) [Remy Martin Cognac Louis XIII Bottle] Retrieved October, 2, 2020, from https://www.wallywine.com/remy-martin-cognac-louis-xiii-750ml.html

Image 10: Tastetomorrow (2017) The power of packaging: how smart can packaging be? ["NFC Labelled" Rémy Martin Bottle] Retrieved October, 2, 2020, from https://www.tastetomorrow.com/media/376/20171205-090238-4-Q4_w52_TT_Article_visual_3%E2%80%93internet_of_packaging.png

CONSUMER

123

Bei Fragen zur Produktsicherheit wenden Sie sich bitte an:
If you have any questions regarding product safety,
please contact:

Walter de Gruyter GmbH
Genthiner Straße 13
10785 Berlin
productsafety@degruyterbrill.com